WEDDINGS
A Celebration

BEVERLY CLARK

WILSHIRE PUBLICATIONS

WILSHIRE PUBLICATIONS
1120A MARK AVENUE
CARPINTERIA, CA 93013
(800) 888–6866

Library of Congress Cataloging Number: 96-61134

Clark, Beverly.
Weddings: A Celebration

ISBN 0-934081-14-X

Printed and bound in Hong Kong

10 9 8 7 6 5 4 3 2

EDITORIAL DIRECTOR: *Millie Szerman*
TEXT EDITOR: *Lynette Padwa*
ART DIRECTOR: *Penelope C. Paine*
PRODUCTION CONSULTANT: *Nick Clemente*
COVER PRODUCTION: *Jon Rosenberg*
BOOK PRODUCTION: *Cirrus Design*

PREVIOUS PAGE: LEFT: *FRED MARCUS PHOTOGRAPHY.* RIGHT: *HEIDI MAURACHER*
THIS PAGE: *HEIDI MAURACHER*

SCOTT A. NELSON

CONTENTS

*This book is dedicated to the talented individuals
in the wedding business who creatively assist the soon-to-be newlyweds
to realize their wedding dreams.*

Acknowledgments

This project could not have been successful without the dedication, hours of hard work and creative energies of so many talented individuals. I knew from the start that I faced an almost overwhelming enterprise, and was delighted with the support and encouragement of all who contributed. Through the months, we experienced both ends of the spectrum—from frustration to exhilaration, and shared in the joys of so many families.

My love and thanks go first to my husband, Nelson, for believing in this project from the very beginning and for all his help at home and in the office. Another special thank you to my children, Lauren and Nicholas, both of whom provided boundless energy and enthusiasm. Their acceptance of my virtual absence was met mostly with humor and goodwill. I am appreciative of Roxanna Curelea who managed to keep everyone in the household from getting underfoot.

I am grateful and most indebted for the dedication of my devoted team of editorial and design experts, who worked so intensely from the onset of this project, through the wee hours of many a morning, right to the very end and without each of them, this book would not have been possible. To Millie Szerman, whose inspiration and commitment to the project was unending, and whose continued sense of humor added levity when we needed it; Christine Nolt, for her amazing patience, incredible computer skills and attention to every detail; Lynette Padwa for her writing talent and unwavering word presence; Penelope Paine, who provided page-by-page artistic direction and who single-handedly kept us all on track; and to Tracy Bettles, for sharing her printing expertise and knack with mailing tape.

And a thank you to our support team: Mary Nadler, Gail Kearns, and Ty Koontz.

I am also indebted to my friends and colleagues for their unwavering support, special contributions, and numerous referrals: Mindy Bingham, Patti Clark, Sunday Hendrickson, Jan Kish, Brian Kramer, Mary Litzsinger, Othene Munson, Joni Papay, Laurel Philips, Ellen Reid, Gary Varney and my friends at Santa Monica Antique Market.

And an extra special thanks go to many extraordinarily talented wedding professionals; the resourceful vision of the photographers, the skillful inspiration of the cake and floral designers, and the artistic invitation stylists and wedding consultants, all of whom generously donated their time and counsel, along with photographic representations of their work. Too numerous to mention here, you will find them listed in our source directory in the back of this book.

Last, but certainly not least, I must thank all the delightful wedding couples, their families and friends, who are featured throughout the pages of *Weddings: A Celebration*.

$\mathcal{I}$NTRODUCTION

BRIAN KRAMER

As far back as I can remember, I knew my wedding day would be a special one. A day filled with excited anticipation, elegance, happiness and, of course, love. It would be a spectacular affair, one that everyone in attendance would always remember, especially me! And it was, not only because I wanted it to be, but because I spent painstaking hours researching special touches that would personalize my wedding and make it unique.

That's what this book is all about. It provides you with information and pictures that will inspire you and spark your own creative imagination. For many months, my staff and I worked with wedding photographers, party planners, bridal consultants, and floral and cake designers, among others. We've gone through thousands of photographs and exhausted countless hours talking to wedding professionals worldwide to bring you the most comprehensive visual presentation of some of the most exclusive and unusual weddings in the world.

In 1986, when I wrote the first edition of *Planning A Wedding to Remember,* it quickly became America's #1 best-selling wedding guidebook, and has since been revised three times to incorporate changes in the lifestyles and points of view of couples today. Since that time I have become fascinated and inspired by the wonderful ways, both elaborate and simple, that we celebrate matrimony.

This new book, *Weddings: A Celebration,* will do more than just help guide you through the process of planning your own distinctive event. As you review the more than 500 photographs, I hope you'll take note of the little things that can make your wedding just that much more memorable—the things that the most elite party planners,

hotel wedding coordinators, and imaginative people in the world have used to highlight their own events.

Please use the ideas shared within these pages to create your own celebration. The book is organized in ten chapters to help you find themes and ideas for your own special day. They include: Wedding Style, Unique Weddings, Invitations and Favors, Celebrations, The Wedding Party, Flowers, The Ceremony, Receptions, Cakes and even Bon Voyage.

Finally, as you embark on your own course of planning, I encourage you to use the source directory where you'll find information of those who so generously gave their time and energy to make this book as beautiful as you see it. And, please, let us know how we've helped you. We'd love to hear from you.

A wedding is truly an exciting time—a day for sharing love, happiness and traditions with the ones closest to you. May I wish you long lasting happiness, now and always. Congratulations!

Beverly Clark

WEDDING STYLE

A WEDDING OCCUPIES a season all its own. There should be a special name for the dizzying journey that begins when you realize you must start making arrangements now, and ends only when you close the door to your honeymoon suite. Never again will your attention be focused so passionately on a single day.

Couples who have experienced the turmoil and delight of a wedding may assail you with advice, but in the end your wedding belongs to you and your groom alone—it will be an expression of your personalities, hopes, and beliefs. The wedding ceremony is a joyous rite of passage, revered as much by modern folk as it was by our distant ancestors. But unlike couples in earlier times, today's engaged couples are free to create weddings that celebrate their individuality. Whether it takes place in a wooded glade or a glittering ballroom, your wedding will give you and your groom the rare chance to share, with your families and friends, your vision of the ultimate romantic fantasy.

No matter how well you think you know yourself and your fiancé, preparing for your wedding will reveal new facets of both of you. A free spirit may suddenly decide that only a traditional church wedding will do. A woman who always assumed her wedding would be a small, family affair will discover that her fiancé longs for an event worthy of Cecil B. DeMille. Religion, family, and childhood dreams all play a part in the creation of a wedding, and each helps set the tone for your wedding style. Such pragmatic concerns as your budget, location, and season need to be considered, as well—there's a direct ratio between how lavish your wedding can be and how many people can attend.

A wedding is a monumental occasion, and it's the rare couple who agree on every aspect of the festivities. But if you allow yourselves time enough to think things through and plan carefully, you can create the wedding of your dreams.

WHAT IS WEDDING STYLE?

The word *style* conjures up slick fashion magazines, designer-perfect settings, unassailable good taste, and unachievable dress sizes. But when it comes to weddings, style means something different from following predetermined formulas. In a wedding, style is personal. The more your wedding reflects your personal interests and tastes, the more naturally your style will unfold. If you prefer pomp and ceremony, you'll glow in a picture-book wedding with a dozen begowned bridesmaids. If you love music, an afternoon ceremony at a music conservatory might capture just the right mood.

When you and your fiancé begin to plan your wedding, start off by thinking of the common interests that brought the two of you together. Whether your interests lie in horses or hiking or movies or travel, let your passions lead the way, and your style will follow. Even in the most traditional of weddings, there are plenty of opportunities to make personal choices: in the colors, the music, the flowers, the food, the cake, and the ceremony itself.

PREVIOUS PAGE: *An elegant reception at the Plaza Hotel.*
PHOTO: *Fred Marcus Photography*

ABOVE: *Cake: Sylvia Weinstock. Photo: Brian Kramer*
OPPOSITE: *Delicate organza laces create elegant pedestal aisle decor.*
PHOTO: *G. Gregory Geiger.*

12

HOW FORMAL SHOULD IT BE?

The first decision you'll need to make in planning your wedding is that of formality. While many couples opt for the traditional event, with a full complement of attendants, more informal weddings are also becoming popular. While informal doesn't necessarily mean less costly, these weddings do offer a greater degree of flexibility in everything from location to attire to cuisine. Formal, semiformal, and informal weddings are all options for today's couples.

FORMAL

Formal weddings are usually held in a church, synagogue, temple, the ballroom of a hotel, or a home or garden (if size allows). These weddings follow a myriad of time-honored customs, preserved down to the last elegant detail. Invitations are traditionally worded and often custom printed; the wedding photographs are carefully orchestrated; the dinner or luncheon is an elaborate sit-down affair or

a generous buffet. Tables bear professionally-designed floral displays and boast a profusion of linens and crystal. A live orchestra or band provides music for the guests.

The formal bridal party consists of four to twelve attendants: a maid or matron of honor, the best man, bridesmaids, one usher for every fifty guests, one or two flower girls, and a ring-bearer. The bride's gown is a work of art, full length, usually with a train and veil. The number of guests is often between 150 and 400 (and may be as high as 800 or more). It's not unusual for the bride and groom to enlist the aid of a wedding consultant in planning these lavish events.

SEMIFORMAL

Some, but not all, of the guidelines are relaxed in

A Fantasy Wedding

Pink roses and white tulle magically converted the Grand Ballroom at the Four Seasons Hotel, Chicago, into a fantasy world for the Newman/Sachs wedding where more than three hundred guests sat in individually decorated chairs, double-wrapped and cleverly fastened with pink roses. Her excitement hidden by her sheer veil, Allyson Brooke Newman is escorted by her delighted Dad, Mark A. Newman. Janet Newman, her mother, carefully undertook all the details to create an enchanted affair for all to remember in honor of her daughter's wedding to Jay Adam Sachs. Even the ballroom walls were covered with silk and tulle, authenticating the theme. Two orchestras played into the wee hours of the morning.

PHOTOS: JOHN REILLY

ABOVE: *Lattice archway creates an engaging frame for this semiformal outdoor wedding. Photo: Monte Clay*
BELOW: *Hanging basket. Photo: Durango Steele.* OPPOSITE: *Photo: Joann Pecoraro*

a semiformal wedding. The ceremony and reception can take place in a variety of locations, and both are often held at the same place. Semiformal weddings usually have fewer attendants, and wedding attire and flowers may be less traditional and more innovative.

Informal

Informal weddings come in all sizes and settings, from a small cluster of friends gathered around a fire in a country lodge to an expansive fete on a rented yacht. Many informal weddings are second marriages, and they often take place in the daytime. Appropriate attire might be a knee- or ankle-length dress or a suit, in white or pastel. The invitation can be anything from a hand-written note to a custom-designed card. Floral arrangements and decorations are optional, but most couples prefer to dress up the setting with flowers, perhaps presented in casual baskets or vases rather than in formal displays. Many informal weddings do not feature full meals. Instead, guests are treated to refreshments such as hor d'oeuvres, punch and cham-pagne, and wedding cake. Or, the couple may choose to host a small, intimate dinner for close friends and family.

TRADITION

Tradition is a broad concept. It can mean family customs or religious practices, ethnic traditions, or customs unique to the part of the country where you were raised. Weddings tap into a longing that many people have to connect with their traditions, and this means

delving into the past. You'll probably find yourself pouring through family photo albums in a search for wedding rituals, food, dress, or decorations that resonate for you. You may find them in the smallest details: the red rosebud tucked into your father's lapel on the morning he married your mother, or the special sugar-dusted wedding cookies your grandmother made for them that day. Perhaps you can have your baker re-create the wedding cake that was the centerpiece of your favorite aunt's

reception. Or maybe you'd like to reach farther back, to decorations and attire your ancestors used in their wedding celebrations.

Many brides want to honor their mother in a special way in the ceremony or the celebration. Carrying your mother's handkerchief is one way to keep her spirit close; another is to walk down the aisle to the same music she did. One groom surprised his bride by having the musicians play the same tune that had accompanied his mother down the aisle—the traditional Hawaiian wedding song.

The "tossing" bouquet is yet another way to honor your mother: it can be designed to look like the one she carried at her own wedding.

A lovely European custom, honored at the Swiss wedding of Isabelle Schneider and Sean McCue, involved baking a large loaf of bread in the shape of two entwined hearts, with the couple's names. Another time-honored tradition has the bride carrying the family heirloom Bible for use during the ceremony. Book-lover Mindy Bingham began a family tradition when she purchased an antique Bible, printed in 1682. She loved the fact that it had been signed by other couples to mark special occasions over the past three hundred years. When she and her groom, Jim Comiskey, signed the Bible on their wedding day, they brought the centuries-old custom into their own family.

An Intimate Affair

Mindy Bingham and Jim Comiskey's private ceremony and reception, held at the charmingly quaint San Ysidro Ranch in Montecito, CA, took place in the late afternoon. The lush garden ceremony was followed by cocktails, and an intimate dinner was served in one of the cozy, full of character, historic adobe dining rooms. Harp melodies provided romantic harmony throughout the day.

An heirloom bible, dating back to 1682, now bears signatures of the bride and groom, carrying on the tradition.

PHOTOS: CLINT WEISMAN

FLOWERS: FLORAMOR STUDIOS PHOTOS: ELIOT HOLTZMAN

Deborah Geller and Roger Reynolds orchestrated a very traditional and quite stunning Jewish wedding at San Francisco's Fairmont Hotel. The Gold Room, a grand setting that easily accommodated the couple's three hundred guests, was the site for both the ceremony and the reception. Crystal chandeliers and sconces, creamy walls detailed in gold, and deep bay windows hung with ivory draperies, provided a backdrop for florist Laura Little's sophisticated decor. Laura and her partner Stephen O'Connell run

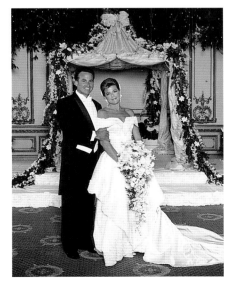

Floramor Studios in San Francisco, specializing in the custom design of weddings. Here, golden vases held artful arrangements of orchids and aromatic roses. Table linens were ivory, accented with pale French ribbons scattered with gold stars.

Large ficus trees twinkling with small lights framed a traditional *chuppah* to which Little had added exquisite garlands of greenery and fresh flowers in shades of white, cream, and blush. During the reception, the *chuppah* sheltered the wedding cake table.

month you choose have an undeniable impact on the tone of the occasion.

RITES OF SPRING

Weddings that take place in March, April, or May have the advantage of being first on the year's wedding dance card. Depending on where you live, March may be an unpredictable month, often bringing winds and rain. April and May are unpredictable, too, but less so. April is an unabashedly romantic month, with many of the year's loveliest flowers. May weddings offer all the benefits of those held in April, plus the likelihood of better weather.

DURANGO STEELE

JOANN PECORARO

DURANGO STEELE

SUMMER WEDDINGS

June, of course, is the most popular month in which to marry. The tradition began centuries ago with the ancient Romans. The month of June was named for Juno, goddess of women and marriage, who vowed to protect those who married in her month. In many areas June is also the first month of predictably fair weather. Another June offering: roses, the quintessential romantic flowers that bloom profusely during this month. And school ends in June, freeing guests to travel and college-age newlyweds to take their honeymoons.

But getting married in June has its challenges, too. Wedding locations, musicians, florists, caterers,

STEPHANIE HOGUE

DENIS REGGIE

and clergy are all in high demand during this month. If many of your friends are also getting married, there could be conflicts among you concerning dates. Being a June bride is worth the extra planning if you've had that particular dream since adolescence, and the month does carry an undeniable joyousness. Just be sure to allow enough time to make arrangements for services you need and want.

For couples who want a summer wedding but are not emotionally bound to the month of June, July is a fine choice. It's the height of summer, nights are long, and outdoor weddings run little risk of bad weather (although humidity can be a formidable problem in some places). Family members who live far away may be more able to get time off from work to travel in summer months, and children are out of school. The same goes for August. It is such a popular vacation month that if you don't send your invitations out well in advance, you might receive a higher-than-usual number of regrets.

PHOTO: G. GREGORY GEIGER FLOWERS: RENNY

PHOTO: G. GREGORY GEIGER FLOWERS: CLARE WEBBER

Fall Is for Lovers

There are numerous good reasons to consider getting married in September or October. The weather is mild and crisp, and the tide of summer travelers has ebbed a bit. In many parts of the country the scenery is spectacular in the fall, making it easier to lure far-flung family and friends to your celebration. Some couples make the autumn foliage a key part of their wedding design, using wreaths, harvest motifs, and a warm, fiery palette in their decorating schemes. Another advantage to autumn weddings: honeymoon destinations are less crowded, since most schools start in September.

Winter Weddings

Fewer people get married in November than in summer or fall, which allows popular wedding locations to be available then. The same holds true for musicians, florists, and caterers, all of whom are eager to spend extra time with you in the slow month before the Christmas holidays.

December is an age-old favorite for nuptials. What is more romantic than exchanging vows in a candlelit chapel, with snow falling outside? The scent of pine in the air, the Yuletide spirit, and the notorious holiday feasting all lend themselves perfectly to a wedding celebration. Many hotels

The bride's gown, as well as her bridesmaids' dresses of red velvet, were designed by her mother and Ursula of Kleinfields. The dance floor was handpainted to replicate ice, complete with an etched-look monogram in the center. Walls were made to look like iced windows covering the exit signs, and the exquiste Sylvia Weinstock cake resembled a floral ice sculpture.

Guests danced to the Gene Donati Orchestra who performed into the wee hours of the morning.

FLOWERS: BARBARA TAYLOR FLORAL DESIGN
PHOTOS: MONTE CLAY

A Russian Winter Wedding Theme

Seasonal colors of red and white roses added a festive touch to the late November wedding of Marci Goodman and Laurence Gottlieb. The bride's mother, Louise Kovens Goodman, independently hosted the elaborate affair held at the renowned Lord Baltimore Hotel, Baltimore, MD, where her parents had been wed a generation earlier.

The Russian Winter Wedding theme was upheld with each and every detail, with the expert assistance of party planner, Sherri D. Minkin. More than 450 roses emphasized each custom-made red velvet tablecloth dotted with rhinestones. Silver frames handsomely designated each place setting and later became favors for the guests to take home.

27

and restaurants are lavishly decorated for the season, so you may be able to save on decorations and still have a festive affair. Families and friends traditionally get together for the holidays, another benefit to planning your wedding at this time. According to Irish folktales, the last day of the year is an especially lucky one on which to wed.

Scottish lore, meanwhile, has it that January 1 is the most fortuitous day for a wedding. Tying the knot in January or February has the same advantages as doing so in November, with many sites and services more readily available to you. These months are also a perfect time for a honeymoon wedding, mentioned in the next chapter. In quiet winter months, family and friends will welcome an invitation to travel to a ski village or an exotic (and possibly warmer) locale. If you're considering a winter wedding, remember that February has the most romantic wedding date of all—Valentine's Day.

ABOVE: *Red poinsettias provide decoration for this winter wedding. Photo: James D. Macari*
BELOW: *A warm glow from a candle-lit window. Photo: Durango Steele*

OPPOSITE: *Nostalgic horsedrawn carriage, appropriately decorated for the Yuletide season. Photo: Madearis Photography Studio*
BELOW: *Flower girl's red plaid dress is a charming complement to a holiday wedding. Photo: Durango Steele*

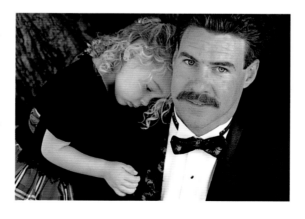

SETTING THE DATE

In addition to the season, a few other key factors need consideration before choosing a wedding date: the size and formality of your wedding, your work or school schedules, and the availability of the location. You'll also need to ask important family members about dates that are convenient for them. Consider the honeymoon too. Is it a good time of year to travel to your dream destination? When you've chosen a tentative date, review the Wedding Calendar Checklist on page 268 and make sure there's enough time to do everything on your list.

If you have your heart set on a location that is popular, reserve it six months to a year ahead of time. With an increase in formal weddings, you'd be surprised how many locations are reserved months in advance. Even if your wedding is small and informal, you should allow three months to plan it; and two at the very least. I recommend such a brief planning period only if you are having a home wedding, getting married during one of the less popular winter months, or perhaps if you are getting married on a weekday.

PLANNING THE WEDDING

In contemplating the myriad details that go into creating a wedding, you may feel a bit overwhelmed. If so, you're not alone. Even the woman who's been planning her wedding since childhood will usually experience a shock wave or two when faced with transforming her dreams into reality. It's definitely a challenge, so before you start setting up meetings, take a little time to focus.

Begin by considering each aspect of your wedding: the ceremony, your gown and your bridesmaids' dresses, the flowers and decorations, the menu, and the music. Peruse the Wedding Calendar Checklist (page 268) to acquaint yourself with all the elements that go into making a wedding. Jot down any ideas, colors, or moods that appeal to you.

Ask your fiancé for his thoughts. He'll enjoy being part of the planning, and can be a great help when it comes to juggling meetings and making decisions. If you need more assistance, your mother is probably eager to help. Ask friends to refer florists, musicians, and caterers. They might find it fun to go

shopping with you, offering their opinions.

What if you're too busy to personally oversee the preparations? In that case you might want to hire a wedding consultant. Consultants are privy to abundant resources and have names and numbers of the best caterers, florists, musicians, and others in your area. The comfort and advice of an expert can be invaluable to you. There are other circumstances, too, in which a bride-to-be might benefit from the services of a consultant. For example, if your wedding will be a large, extravagant affair, you may quickly discover that you don't have the logistical expertise to handle all the plans yourself. Or perhaps you don't want to handle them; maybe organization has never been your strong suit. Perhaps your wedding will take place in another city, and you won't get a chance to visit every site and interview every vendor yourself. No matter what your situation, hiring a consultant will free you to spend more time with your family, friends, and fiancé in the exciting months prior to your wedding day.

UNIQUE WEDDINGS

NOT SO LONG AGO, wedding location choices were simple: a church or temple, the grand ballroom of a luxury hotel, or a private home were places where couples got married. Today, the sky's the limit, and even some adventurous couples actually take their vows while aloft in hot-air balloons. Anything goes, and more so if your wedding will be an informal one.

The location you choose to set your ceremony and reception provides the foundation for your wedding style. Once you've made that crucial decision, you can start to compile the guest list, consider the music and flowers, and all the other details. If yours is to be a theme wedding, your site will help bring your vision to life. The great hall of a rented mansion is ideal for a Renaissance theme, while

PREVIOUS PAGE: *A flashback to the Old West! Western style wedding, designed by Scott Hogue, rides into the San Ysidro Ranch, Montecito, CA. Outdoor seats, adorned with sunflowers, eucalyptus sprays and raffia ribbon along with bales of hay, establish the wedding aisle.*
PHOTOS: *Durango Steele*

ABOVE: *Call the sheriff! Groom steals a kiss!*
PHOTO: *Durango Steele*

ABOVE CENTER AND BELOW: *Cheerful blue and white gingham emphasizes the western theme on tables and food stations.*

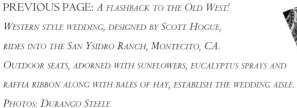

ABOVE: *Bride and groom take a moment to pose by this rustic wagon.*
PHOTO: *Jennifer Drake*

LEFT CENTER: *The western-themed invitation, embellished with glitter and raffia bows by Ann Fiedler, launched the affair.*
PHOTO: *Michael Garland*

BELOW CENTER: *Magnificent fringed wedding cake, topped with his and her cowboy hats and trimmed with edible silver studs by Jan Kish, continued the theme.*

BELOW: *Jan Kish's chili decorated mints and confectionery boot-shaped place cards provide an extra special touch to this wild west wedding.*
PHOTOS: *Lambert Photography*

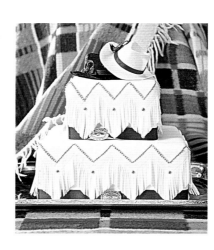

32

carefully cultivated museum gardens would perfectly frame an afternoon Victorian wedding. The place of the ceremony has a ripple effect on the rest of the celebration. Most ceremonies are still

religious affairs, so couples typically begin at their church or synagogue. The reception site must be within an easy drive, unless your place of worship has party facilities on the premises.

Delightful decorations created with sunflowers, saddles and western artifacts by Joni Papay of Hearts Bloom.
Photos: Mark Papay

G. GREGORY GEIGER

PRIVATE HOMES OR GARDENS

There's a special warmth and personality unique to the home wedding. The event can be a formal, catered affair or an informal ceremony and do-it-yourself reception.

Size is the crucial factor in considering a home or garden wedding. Couples these days are opting to take their home wedding outdoors, with the help of a rented tent. More guests can be included this way, and the house is spared the intense makeover that a wedding usually demands. Inventive brides have used potted trees and flowering plants, twinkle lights, candles, floating bunches of helium-filled

ABOVE: Beautiful, ageless garden oak trees frame bride and her attendants. Photos: Durango Steele

balloons trailing ribbons, swaths of tulle or muslin, and even props from theatrical companies to transform tents into magical, romantic spaces. A wooden dance floor or small stage can be brought in.

If the ceremony will be held in a home, envision the most effective place to stage it. Perhaps you can descend from a staircase and exchange vows in front of a large picture window. A ceremony held in front of a fireplace, especially if it's winter and the fire is aglow, is bound to be memorable. Indoor ceremonies have limited space for guests unless your home is quite large, but if the ceremony is brief, guests can stand.

Couples who plan to exchange vows in the garden might hold the ceremony under a stately old tree or a decorated arch or gazebo. Try to position it so the sun will not shine in your guests' eyes during the ceremony. Depending on space and your ceremony length, you may choose to have your guests seated or standing (again, for a short ceremony only). When you're planning an outside ceremony, make sure that the area can be tented or the ceremony moved indoors in the event of bad weather.

If your home isn't large enough, perhaps a friend or relative would offer the use of theirs. Private homes to rent are often available through real-estate agencies, wedding consultants, or local newspapers. Location and site search firms may be able to point you toward such a space.

LEFT: *Magnificent circular stairway decorated with floral garlands presents a dramatic entrance for any bride. Photo: Clay Blackmore*

OPPOSITE: *Tiny twinkle lights and elaborate ribbon decor strung from the ceiling turn this ordinary tent into a magical locale. Pink colors are reflected in elegant floral centerpieces. Photo: Brian Kramer*

Private Clubs

Private clubs are lovely settings, but few open their doors to non-members. If your family does not have a membership in a club whose facilities you covet, consider your circle of acquaintances: perhaps you have a relative or close friend who would be honored to host (not pay for) your wedding. Private clubs often have exquisite banquet rooms and lush grounds—many are situated at the edge of a golf course. They offer most of the same amenities as hotels, and their atmosphere is a bit more private.

Hotels

A hotel can be a glorious setting particularly for a formal wedding. In terms of style, hotels have some distinct advantages. The staff personnel are pros at staging large events, and equipment is usually available everyday—from dance floors to chairs and tables to salad forks. They can usually

FRED MARCUS PHOTOGRAPHY

accommodate hundreds of guests and easily house both the ceremony and the reception. Many hotels will furnish altars, aisle runners, and canopies. Larger hotels will insist on supplying the food, while smaller boutique hotels or bed-and-breakfast inns may allow you to bring in your own caterer. Popular hotels will book up rapidly, especially in the traditionally busy wedding months of summer, so make your reservations early.

Before committing to a specific hotel, find out exactly what your contract includes at what prices. Call a rental company to research availability and cost of any extras your hotel is unable to provide. Make sure the venue gives you enough time to set up, celebrate, and then clear out your flowers, gifts, and guests. Some hotels allow only five hours and will charge additional fees if you go beyond that limit. Everything is negotiable, so try to make extended hours part of your initial agreement.

FRED MARCUS PHOTOGRAPHY

DURANGO STEELE

MOUNTAINS, PARKS, AND BEACHES

In the 1970s, young people started a trend: the nature wedding, held not in a tidy garden but in the great outdoors. Once considered offbeat, this type of wedding now typically includes all the traditional rituals. The setting adds a touch of adventure to the celebration. What could be more romantic than saying your vows under an azure sky, to the music of ocean waves?

Your parks and recreation department can help find the perfect spot for your outdoor ceremony. City and state parks usually have a wide range of sites, from formal gardens to rustic, fern-covered canyons.

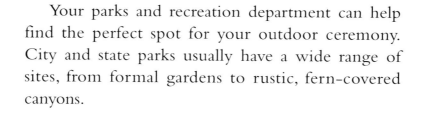

ABOVE RIGHT: *Sandy beach nuptials. Photo: Heidi Mauracher*

ALL OTHERS: *Seaside embraces. Photos: Durango Steele*

SHIPS AND BOATS

Waterborne weddings are gaining favor in areas where a lake, river, or the ocean plays a prominent role in the landscape and lore. Riverboats on the Mississippi, *Love Boat* cruise ships off the coast of San Diego, and chartered yachts breezing down southern Florida's intercoastal waterways all make for unforgettable wedding sites. Weddings held aboard ships can be as formal as those held in a fancy ballroom or as casual as a picnic.

If you'd like a waterborne wedding but don't own a boat, check the Yellow Pages in your area for rentals. Prices will vary according to the size of the vessel and the number of hours you'll be on board. In most cases, you will provide the catered food, whether it be an elaborate buffet dinner or simply cake and coffee. Cruise ships offer their own catering services.

ALL HANDS ON DECK FOR THE FUN-LOVING NAUTICAL WEDDING AND RECEPTION FOR DANA SERIGHT AND JOHN HEYMAN. PHOTOS: SCOTT A. NELSON

THIS NAUTICAL THEME WEDDING CAKE DECORATED WITH EDIBLE GOLD ROPE IS CLEVERLY DISPLAYED ON WOOD PILINGS.
PHOTO: SCOTT A. NELSON

*Up, up and away, an
adventurous couple tie the
knot in mid-air.*
Photos: Clark Crouse

WINERIES

Many wineries are lovely old buildings nestled in rolling, vine-covered hills—a beautiful setting for a unique wedding. Several rent their facilities, but prices vary widely, so investigate before making a decision. Remember, wine country gets hot in the summer. Spring and fall are the best months for winery weddings.

In California's Napa Valley, as elsewhere in the nation, hot-air balloons have entered the wedding scene in a big way. Couples can plan an early morning ceremony—aboard the balloon, if they like—then float to the winery to meet their guests for a champagne brunch reception.

SCOTT A. NELSON

HEARTS BLOOM

BRIAN KRAMER

HISTORICAL OR PUBLIC SITES

A grand old plantation house, an elegant flagstone mansion, a breathtaking mountain lodge. . . there are hundreds of magnificent homes that have been donated over the years to cities or states and can be rented for weddings. If you've always wanted to live in the world of Gatsby or Scarlett, this is your chance. Museums, arboretums, and formal gardens also make for beautiful or whimsical settings. There are even a few castles, both in the United States and abroad, that will open their doors to a wedding celebration.

SCOTT A. NELSON

Grand Settings

If you've ever dreamed of being married in a castle, these regal settings await you and your wedding party. Some locations, including castles, manor houses and country estates are available through Gatehouse Travel for your exclusive use.

ABOVE CENTER: *Skibo Castle, Northern Highlands, Scotland*

CENTER LEFT: *The Manor House, Castle Combe, classic English grandeur in the beautiful Cotswolds, England*

BELOW LEFT: *The enchanting Crabtree and Evelyn bedroom at the stately Stapleford House, near Leicester, England.*

CENTER RIGHT: *Horsted Place in Uckfield, one of England's finest estates and country homes.*

BELOW RIGHT: *Elegant dining room at Stapleford House.*

OPPOSITE: *Dating back to Tudor times, Hever Castle and village provide a unique "Olde English" experience.*

Brooklyn Museum: Florals by Ron Wendt Design. Photos: G. Gregory Geiger

- *Wineries, ranches, or orchards*
- *Bed-and-breakfast inns*
- *Romantic restaurants*
- *Hotel ballrooms*
- *University chapels*
- *Churches or synagogues*
- *Yachts, boats, barges*
- *Romantic resorts*
- *Military club facilities*

WEDDING LOCATIONS

Listed below are popular choices that may not have occurred to you. To find more locations, check local newspapers and phone books or call the Chamber of Commerce in your area.

- *Private clubs*
- *Civic or private theaters*
- *Art galleries*
- *Museums*
- *Historic buildings or mansions*
- *Community centers*
- *Private homes or estates*
- *Public beaches, parks, or gardens*
- *Zoos or amusement parks*
- *Movie studio lots*

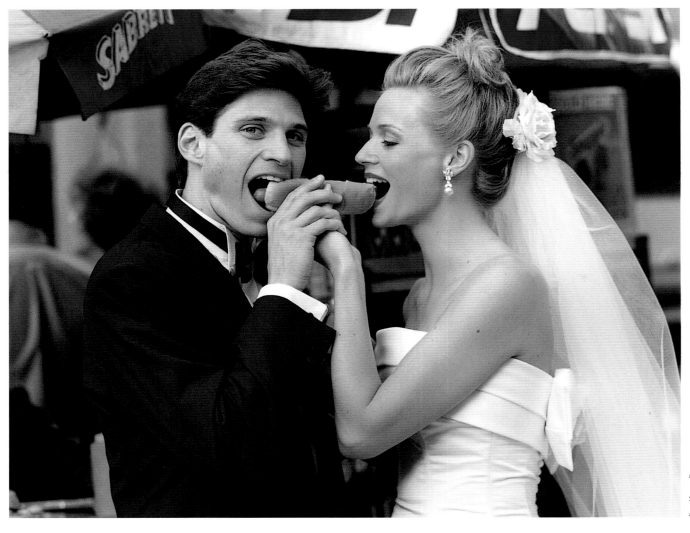

FRED MARCUS PHOTOGRAPHY

THEME WEDDINGS

For some brides and grooms, the fantasy doesn't stop with a princess gown or flower-covered arbor.

Some couples want to create a whole world on their wedding day and give their guests an experience they'll never forget. They may take their cue from a favorite historical era, putting on elaborate affairs with all the trappings of Edwardian England or medieval France. Still others may opt for a nostalgic, turn-of-the-century Americana theme.

PORTRAITS BY TONY

After exchanging their vows in the gazebo of a shady park, they might treat their guests to an old-fashioned picnic reception, giving each guest their own picnic basket stuffed with delicacies. Western weddings are perennial favorites. They're usually held outdoors, where revelers can enjoy the open skies, children can take pony rides, and a country band can play as loud and long as the crowd demands.

A Victorian Wedding

Mary Litzsinger, owner of Vintage Productions, makes her living turning wedding fantasies into reality. "We'll re-create an era right down to the sawdust on the floor or the bustles on the ladies' skirts."

Historic authenticity is a point of pride for couples who want a theme wedding. Victorian settings are especially popular. Allison-Claire Acker researched and designed the bridal attire, right down to her selected vintage accessories, for her Victorian wedding to Timothy Francis Sylvester. They hired a dance instructor to teach them a Victorian waltz, which was the first dance at their reception. The guests at this particular fête joined in the costume spirit: one pair came as chimney sweeps, while another guest arrived as an Indian Raj, visiting from the farthest reaches of the British Empire.

PHOTOS: CHUCK GARDNER PHOTOGRAPHY

A FESTIVE RENAISSANCE WEDDING

The Renaissance wedding is another favorite theme. It often features sporting games, musicians strumming lutes and dulcimers, and brilliantly colored costumes. A Renaissance-style bridal gown laces up the back of the bodice and looks especially beautiful when the bride and groom are standing at the altar. Other period details from the Renaissance include elaborate headpieces, flower arrangements with flowing greenery, and of course, tights for the men. A master reveler can set the tone of the celebration by announcing the arrival of the bride and groom and the activities of the day. A dance mistress might instruct the guests in various period dances.

MANNING PARK, MONTECITO, CA, WAS THE SETTING FOR A RENAISSANCE EXTRAVAGANZA CREATED BY MARY LITZSINGER OF VINTAGE PRODUCTIONS, WITH FLOWERS BY HEARTS BLOOM'S JONI PAPAY. CUSTOM-DESIGNED COSTUMES FOR THE BRIDE AND GROOM AND GUESTS ADDED TO THE GAIETY OF THE EVENT WHICH INCLUDED A FANCIFUL FEAST, COMPETITIVE GAMES, LIVELY DANCING, AND MERRY MINSTRELS AND JUGGLERS. PHOTOS: GLENDA BACON-CARTER

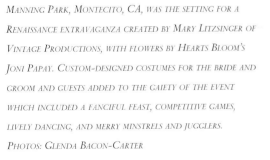

ABOVE: *Superbly coordinated outfits grace this delightful Elizabethan wedding. The groom and his ushers are especially dashing in their high boots and knickers. Photo: Brian Kramer*

LEFT: *Another Elizabethan favorite, this wedding featured a dance around the May Pole. Flowers: Hearts Bloom. Photo: Mark Papay*

INVITATIONS BY ROCK SCISSOR PAPER

THE FLYING LINDY HOPPERS

1940s SUPPER CLUB WEDDING

Richard Plotkin and Ryan Patterson of Los Angeles had their hearts set on a 1940s jazz wedding. To provide the setting, Vintage Productions transformed a historic theater into a jazz-age dinner club. The musicians, Big Bad Voodoo Daddy, decked out in zoot suits, spent the evening regaling the crowd with big-band and swing-era tunes. The Flying Lindy Hoppers, a 1940s style swing-dance group, performed and instructed guests. A costumed cigarette girl circulated among the tables, handing out candy cigarettes, matchbooks, and banded cigars, bearing the names of the bride and groom. A magician entertained while a photo girl snapped Polaroids of guests at their tables and slipped the pictures into custom photo jackets as take-home favors. Silent black and white clips of old movies and TV shows were projected on the screen as guests celebrated. The cake was an Art Deco masterpiece.

If you're intrigued by the idea of a theme wedding but aren't sure what fantasy to pursue, take a trip to the video store. Movies such as *The Great Gatsby, The Age of Innocence, Immortal Beloved, Restoration,* and *High Society* offer detailed glimpses into the elegant styles of days gone by.

ABOVE CENTER: *PERIOD LAMPS PROVIDED BY VINTAGE PRODUCTIONS. MIRRORED BASES WITH FRAGRANT WHITE GARDENIA CENTERPIECES DESIGNED BY HEARTS BLOOM. PHOTO: MARK PAPAY* ALL OTHER PHOTOS: *SCOTT STREBLE*

A snowy mountain slope, at 16,000 feet, in picturesque Aspen, offered the ideal setting for this adventuresome couple. Anita Howe-Waxman and Al Waxman along with family members and guests arrived together on snow mobiles for nuptials performed under a chuppah held up by ski poles! Guests attending the "apres ski" reception, held in a tent, were treated to buffalo burgers, elk stew, caviar and champagne.

PHOTOS: STEPHANIE RAE PHOTOGRAPHY. BLACK-AND-WHITE PHOTO: TOMMY NEWIRTH

NEW WAYS TO WED

Modern brides and grooms are innovators, daring to add new twists to the old traditions of marriage. Their weddings reflect changing times as they celebrate older couples, second marriages, blended families, and unions that bring together different faiths or cultures. These couples are expanding the traditional boundaries of the wedding while honoring its original purpose: to vow one's faith before a gathering of the tribes.

DURANGO STEELE

THE WEEKEND WEDDING

Because so many couples are no longer marrying in their hometowns, the weekend wedding has become extremely popular. Guests often travel thousands of miles to take part in the celebration, and a weekend full of parties and activities rather than a single event makes their journey all the more worthwhile.

One appealing aspect of the weekend wedding is that it gives the bride and groom some breathing room—time to visit with friends and family. In most weddings it's understood that the newlyweds will spend just a few precious moments with each table of guests, then rush off to the next table, and finally depart for the honeymoon. With a full weekend to enjoy, the pressure is lifted so they can spend more time with friends they rarely get a chance to see.

AN EXCLUSIVE PEBBLE BEACH RESORT PROVIDED THE PERFECT WEEKEND WEDDING GET-AWAY FOR THE BRIDE, THE GROOM AND THEIR GUESTS, WHO HAD THE TIME OF THEIR LIVES.

THIS PAGE: *PHOTOS: DURANGO STEELE*

A weekend wedding does not have to be prohibitively expensive, especially if you give others a chance to get involved. If you have access to a pool, host a poolside barbecue. Take a picnic to the beach or a park. If the weather is gloomy and you can't venture outdoors, hire a cartoonist, astrologer, or magician to entertain your guests. Be sure to canvass friends and relatives for ideas; if someone is particularly enthusiastic about a suggestion, enlist that person to take charge of the activity. Such a hands-on contribution makes a wonderful wedding gift.

Guests will need plenty of time to plan for this fun-filled weekend, so send a preliminary itinerary or announcement well in advance of the actual wedding invitation. As the date approaches, send a schedule of the activities and parties that are planned. Mention any additional costs guests might incur for an activity, and suggest appropriate attire: shorts, jeans, bathing suits, or formal wear. Include information on travel or lodging arrangements. Even though guests are responsible for their own travel and hotel costs, you might try to reserve a group of rooms at a reduced rate.

A WEEKEND WEDDING AGENDA

There is no set formula for planning a weekend full of activities other than trying to arrange diversions most of your guests will enjoy. Some groups have a large contingent of sports fans, while other clans would prefer to visit local museums or historical points of interest.

ABOVE: *This cowboy boot makes the perfect centerpiece with yellow sunflowers. Flowers by Hearts Bloom Photo: Mark Papay*

BELOW: *Horse-drawn carriages take the wedding party and guests to the reception. Photo: Brian Kramer*

An Aspen Weekend Wedding

Lisa Beth Fleck and Bruce Quackenbush chose Aspen, Colorado as the site of a four-day wedding extravaganza. Both sets of parents live in Florida, but Lisa's spend part of each year in the charming Rocky Mountain ski town.

The Labor Day weekend festivities kicked off with a Friday morning breakfast at Shlomo's, a much-loved Aspen deli. Later in the day, the bridesmaids were treated to an elegant luncheon at the Little Nell Hotel. That evening, everyone wandered over to the landmark Jerome Hotel for a western-style barbecue and hoedown. The decor played up the western theme: tables draped with black-and-white checked cloths held single cowboy boots stuffed with yellow daisies. Guests were decked out in full cowboy regalia—denim skirts, bright red bandannas, chaps, ten-gallon hats, and a few even wore leather holsters.

The next day featured a golf tournament, the wedding rehearsal, and a rehearsal dinner hosted by Bruce's parents. After dinner, the guests danced the night away at the Caribou Club.

Sunday was the wedding day, and with the ceremony slated for six o'clock, guests had all day to relax and prepare for the evening's revelry. After a moving interfaith ceremony at Aspen Community Church Chapel (Lisa is Jewish, Bruce is Episcopalian) the wedding party and guests climbed aboard vintage cars and buses for a procession down the streets of Aspen to the Ritz-Carlton Hotel, serenaded all the way by Scottish bagpipers. After hours spent feasting and dancing to big band tunes with their guests, Lisa and Bruce slipped off to the hotel's honeymoon suite, then flew to Hawaii for their honeymoon. Aspen had much to offer guests who decided to linger for a day or two—but nothing to rival Lisa and Bruce's weekend wedding.

PHOTOS: BRIAN KRAMER

THE HONEYMOON WEDDING

The honeymoon wedding is a combination wedding, honeymoon, and reunion. Guests are invited to travel to a romantic vacation spot to enjoy a few days of fun with the bride and groom. This type of event is especially well-suited for couples who have children from previous marriages. It allows the kids to feel included and gives everyone a chance to better know one another.

Other couples opt for a honeymoon wedding because it allows them to keep the celebration small and intimate, while hosting the wedding in their hometown may necessitate inviting a large number of guests. If your budget allows, however, there is nothing to prevent you from hosting as large and as formal a wedding away as you would have at home.

Your budget will depend on the size of the reception and other parties or dinners you choose to host. With the exception of younger children or older parents who may not be able to afford the trip on their own, guests generally pay for their own airfare and accommodations. If a large number of people will be attending, you should check airlines and hotels for group rates. In many cases, the guests stay only a few days; the newlyweds may remain for a longer time or travel to another location before returning home.

THE SURPRISE WEDDING

This is a perfect celebration for couples who don't want family and friends to make a fuss or feel obligated to send a gift. Plenty of people choose to forego the glamour of a traditional wedding: couples who are marrying for a second time; young couples who can't afford a lavish affair but want a big party; or people whose circumstance, for whatever reason, makes a traditional wedding undesirable.

Usually, both the bride and groom are in on the secret. However, if the groom is confident and daring, he may decide to surprise the bride with a proposal and ceremony at the same time. This is not a route I would ordinarily recommend, simply because most women take great pleasure in planning their weddings. It's the rare bride who would appreciate this type of surprise, no matter how eager she is to marry the groom.

The spontaneity of the surprise wedding ceremony turns the event into an emotional and festive occasion for all. The couple may host the party themselves under the pretense of a birthday, housewarming, or no-special-occasion party. Or they may enlist the help of a friend who appears to be "just having a party."

HONEYMOON DESTINATIONS

❧ *A tropical location, such as Hawaii, Bermuda, the Caribbean, Mexico, or Puerto Rico.*

❧ *A cruise ship, riverboat, or a private yacht.*

❧ *A train trip such as the Orient Express.*

❧ *For nature lovers: a dude ranch, a camping trip, or a houseboat rental.*

❧ *A ski resort in the United States or abroad.*

❧ *A cultural experience, to a foreign country such as Egypt, Israel, Greece, or Japan.*

❧ *If your budget is unlimited, you could even charter a plane and fly your guests to a castle in England or Scotland! There are wedding and travel consultants who specialize in making this type of arrangement.*

SURPRISE WEDDING IDEAS

❧ *Host a Halloween costume party where you and your fiancé come dressed as bride and groom; invite the officiant to dress appropriately.*

❧ *Invite guests to a black-tie New Year's Eve party. Recite vows just before midnight.*

❧ *Have guests arrive at your home for what they think is a party. Offer them a glass of champagne, then direct them to waiting limousines or horse-drawn carriages that will take them to the church for a surprise ceremony.*

❧ *Plan a trip or vacation with a group of close friends. Then surprise all by getting married on the trip, turning the event into a honeymoon wedding.*

OPPOSITE: *Photo: Brian Kramer*

Happy occasions are meant to be
shared with family and friends
Fran and Mannie Fineman
invite you to join them in the ceremony
uniting their daughter
Debra Levy
and
Scott Dveris
son of Judy Dveris and Stan Dveris
Saturday, the second of December
Nineteen hundred and ninety-five
at six o'clock in the evening
The Peninsula Hotel
Beverly Hills, California

_and Mrs. Robert Alfred Haley
_st the honour of your presence
_ marriage of their daughter
Constance
to
_r. John Simmons
_ the eleventh of October
_undred and ninety five
_clock in the evening
_ Episcopal church

Charles Parkins

Jayne Frances He_
and
Lance Herbert Anc_
together with their famil_
invite you to join in the cere_
and celebration of their ma_
Friday evening, the sixteenth _
Nineteen hundred and nine_
at Seven o'clock
Christ the King Cha_
Pleasant Hill Califor_
Reception
immediately following the ce_
Lafayette Park Hotel
Lafayette Park California

_request the pleasure of your company
at the marriage of his daughter
Lori Lux
to
Mr. Jeffrey David Woodward
Saturday, the _
Nineteen hundred _
South _

The favour of a reply is reques_
If attending please inclu_

Susan Ladner
and

Myra's Jack

Love fills a lifetime
lifetime begins this _

Mr and Mrs George Alfred R_ Junior
Mr and Mrs Warren Jackson Budges
request the honour of your presence
at the marriage of
their daughter
Krista Marie Budges
to
Mr Philip Todd Burruss
Saturday, the twentieth of April
eighteen hundred and ninety six
at five o'clock
Morningside Baptist Church
_ Piedmont Avenue Northeast
Atlanta Georgia

Black tie optional

INVITATIONS AND FAVORS

THE WEDDING INVITATION is your guests first hint of the festivities that lie ahead. Playful or formal, handwritten by the bride's mother or engraved by Tiffany's, the invitation sets the tone of your wedding and will be a treasured keepsake in the years to come. Fashions in invitations have blossomed over the last decade with trends at both ends of the spectrum, from an expression of your personal taste to the gracious nod of tradition.

Many of today's brides opt for formal wording on their invitations, but fewer are restricting themselves to the classic white or cream-colored paper with black ink. There are many lovely choices available, including handmade papers pressed with leaves and flowers, delicate rice paper and lush, imported cotton rag. There are typefaces to reflect every

Gold-embossed, elegant white leather photo album with complementary Wedding Memories book and guest book. Beverly Clark Collection

taste and temperament. Browsing the samples in a stationery store, particularly if it's a smaller, custom shop, is an aesthetic delight. It's a good idea to establish a few guidelines before you go shopping. The size of the guest list and the style of your wedding are your primary concerns.

THE GUEST LIST

Invitations should be ordered at least three months prior to the wedding to allow time for delivery to you, addressing, and mailing. You should send your invitations out four to six weeks before your wedding date. Therefore, the guest list must be drawn up rather early in the wedding schedule. Everyone who will have a say—the bride and groom, their parents, and perhaps other immediate family members—should compile a list of names, complete with addresses and phone numbers. To

insure that you'll get all the information you need, you may want to create a fill-in-the-blank style form, photocopy it, and hand out stacks of the forms to each of those making a list.

Deciding on the number of guests takes careful thought and diplomacy. This begins when you and your fiancé sit down together to talk about your wedding style. Do you want a large gathering attended by everyone you know, or would you prefer to keep the celebration small and intimate? Think about your budget and the type of party you want. Would you rather invite fewer guests to an elegant sit-down dinner with an open bar, or be able to invite more people and have a less elaborate reception? Consider the site as well. If you have your heart set on a certain location for the ceremony or reception, your guest list may be determined by the maximum number of people allowed in that venue.

In some weddings, each family invites half the guests. This is most common when the bride and groom are from the same hometown and the wedding will take place there. Otherwise, it's usually the bride's family who hosts the wedding in their hometown, and they will likely invite more guests. It's not uncommon to split the guest list in thirds, with the couple providing one-third and each set of parents providing one-third. Ultimately, a sense of fairness should rule the day. Many issues—who is paying for what, whose family is larger, who lives in town—come into play when dividing the guest list. Today, if the groom's family list is extensive, they may offer to help with the wedding expenses.

Invitations should be sent not only to the guests on the list but also to your fiancé's immediate family, your wedding officiant, your wedding attendants, and their spouses or dates if you want to invite them as well.

You probably won't be able to invite everyone you'd like to your wedding celebration, often because of space or budgetary limitations. As you decide on your final guest list, keep in mind that there will always be a few people who won't be able to attend. It's reasonable to expect 10 to 25 percent of your out-of-town guests to send regrets.

Since emotions are volatile at this time, and you may find it necessary to trim your list, understand that sensitive diplomacy is best. Excluding business or casual acquaintances is just one way to pare the number of guests. Children are another, though some couples feel that youngsters add gaiety to the occasion. If you prefer your wedding to be a mostly grown-up affair, make your intentions clear at the onset. It may not be enough just to leave childrens' names off the invitation. To be sure there is no misunderstanding, personally (and gently) inform parents that you are not able to accommodate children. If some of your out-of-town guests are bringing their children, you may want to arrange for child care.

Make a master list of those to whom you will send invitations, and a second list to whom you'll send an announcement. Announcements are only sent to those who will not be invited to the wedding. Arrange each list alphabetically. If you have a computer, use the word-processing program to help you reduce the time spent juggling names.

BLESSINGS FOR POSTERITY

If you are Catholic, you may want to send an invitation to the Pope. Ask your priest how this might be arranged. A papal blessing, which can be framed and cherished forever, may be sent to you.

No matter what your religion, you might decide to send an invitation to the President of the United States. You're likely to receive a beautiful response, blessing your marriage, signed by the President and First Lady. This makes a wonderful keepsake.

LEFT: *Traditional printed invitation. Photo: Madearis Photography Studio*
BELOW: *Bride's File helps organize and fine-tune your guest and gift lists.*
Beverly Clark Collection.

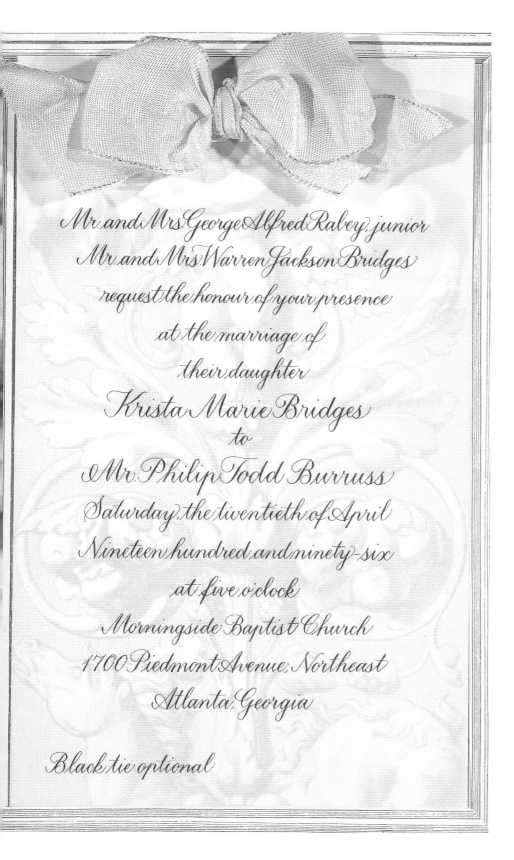

Mr. and Mrs. George Alfred Raley, junior
Mr. and Mrs. Warren Jackson Bridges
request the honour of your presence
at the marriage of
their daughter
Krista Marie Bridges
to
Mr. Philip Todd Burruss
Saturday, the twentieth of April
Nineteen hundred and ninety-six
at five o'clock
Morningside Baptist Church
1700 Piedmont Avenue, Northeast
Atlanta, Georgia

Black tie optional

THE INVITATION

Your invitation should reflect the style of your wedding, but within those parameters there is a lot of room to be creative. Formal wedding invitations were once limited to white or cream-colored cotton rag, engraved with black ink (no thermography for purists). Nowadays, even a very formal affair can be heralded by an invitation that is whimsical, awash in brilliant colors, or artfully sophisticated.

In recent years, I've witnessed nothing short of a revolution in invitation design. Perhaps this is because today's designers are exceptionally creative, or because the burst of innovation in weddings themselves has had a ripple effect on the invitations. I've collected a drawerful of these small master-pieces, and each time I look through them, I'm amazed by their beauty and variety.

The formal invitation has become ever more elaborate. One of my favorites has an intricate seashell scene printed in gold on a cream-colored card, then overlaid with a translucent vellum sheet on which the wording is printed in gold calligraphy. All is tied with a bow of French ribbon in a soft, metallic weave that holds its shape even through the mail.

Papers embedded with flowers and leaves have become very popular, as has the square envelope that unfolds like an origami box. One invitation I treasure features a miniature sculpted cherub, molded of pressed paper. Some invitations come wrapped: the card is slipped inside a folded sheet of delicate tissue or rice paper, then fastened with a pressed flower, a satin bow, or a wax seal made from the family crest.

Bows, seals, and flowers reflect the biggest change in invitation design—the addition of decorations to what was once a simple sheet of card stock.

We invite you to share the joy of our marriage
Please join us Saturday, the fourth of December
nineteen hundred ninety three
one o'clock in the afternoon
Teresa B. Rankin
and
Brett D. Bittle
The Ritz Carlton, 4750 Amelia Island Parkway
Amelia Island Florida
Reception immediately following ceremony
716-655-2935

Some artists specialize in dressing up invitations with raffia, glitter, or confetti—whatever it takes to announce that this celebration is no ordinary event. And color is welcome; many a lovely invitation is printed with colorful flowers, fruit baskets, botanical etchings, or whatever the bride may fancy.

ABOVE: *Calligrapher, Margaret Di Piazza, uses luxuriant handmade papers to accentuate her hand-lettered and letter-press printing. Her custom designs include pre-party and wedding invitations, place cards and flower cones.*

OPPOSITE: *Artistically designed invitation, by Anna Griffin, utilizes an antique gold-printed card with a gold-inscribed vellum overlay, tied together with an ivory colored French wired ribbon.*

The honour of your presence
is requested at the marriage of
Victoria Whyte
to
Stephen H. Ricci, Jr.
Saturday, the twenty-seventh of August
Nineteen hundred and ninety-four
at three o'clock
The Music Academy of the West
1050 Fairway Road
Santa Barbara, California
Reception immediately following

HEIDI MAURACHER

WORDING

Traditionally, the bride's parents host the wedding and are the ones who request either the "honour of your presence" or "the pleasure of your company" on the invitation. "Honor" is used for a religious ceremony, while "pleasure" is reserved for nonreligious celebrations. Listing the bride and her family first is a custom that began long ago when marriages were arranged. A bride was considered the property of her father, and before anyone would attend the wedding, her father had to declare publicly that he was "giving her away."

Dramatic shifts in the modern family have prompted numerous changes in the wording of wedding invitations. Divorced and single parents, remarried parents, blended families, and second marriages all call for different solutions. Keep in

TRADITIONAL INVITATION

Traditional invitation wording reads like this:

Mr. and Mrs. George Allan Craven

request the honour of your presence

at the marriage of their daughter

Susan Claire

to

Mr. James Scott Newman

Saturday, the sixth of June

Nineteen hundred and ninety-eight

at four o'clock

First Presbyterian Church

Santa Barbara, California

mind that the invitation is not the appropriate place to credit everyone who contributed funds to the event; in some cases, the person hosting the wedding may not be the one paying for it. When both sets of parents are hosting the celebration, however, you should consider including the groom's parents on the invitation. If divorced parents or step-parents are hosting, keep the wording clear and simple. A few examples follow, and your stationer can probably show you others.

COMBINED CEREMONY AND RECEPTION INVITATION

This example also includes the response or R.S.V.P. at the bottom. A separate response card may be sent in place of this, if you prefer.

> *Mr. and Mrs. George Alan Craven*
> *request the honour of your presence*
> *at the marriage of their daughter*
> *Susan Claire*
> *to*
> *Mr. James Scott Newman*
> *Saturday, the sixth of June*
> *Nineteen hundred and ninety-eight*
> *at four o'clock*
> *First Presbyterian Church*
> *Santa Barbara, California*
> *Reception*
> *immediately following the ceremony*
> *Biltmore Hotel*
>
> *R.S.V.P.*
> *300 Valley Lane*
> *Santa Barbara, California 93108*

ONE DIVORCED UNMARRIED PARENT HOSTS

When the Bride's unmarried mother hosts, she uses her maiden and married name.

> *Mrs. Lillian Jones Craven*
> *requests the honour of your presence*
> *at the marriage of her daughter*
> *Susan Claire*
> *to*
> *Mr. James Scott Newman*
> *Saturday, the sixth of June*
> *at four o'clock*
> *First Presbyterian Church*
> *Santa Barbara, California*

When the bride's unmarried father hosts:

> *Mr. George Alan Craven*
> *requests the honour of your presence*
> *at the marriage of his daughter*

TWO REMARRIED PARENTS HOST

If the bride's parents are divorced, and both have remarried, but wish to co-host the wedding, the names should appear with the mother's name first.

> *Mr. and Mrs. John Sutton*
> *and*
> *Mr. and Mrs. George Alan Craven*
> *request the honour of your presence*
> *at the marriage of*
> *Susan Claire Craven*
> *to*
> *James Scott Newman*
> *Saturday, the sixth of June*
> *at four o'clock*
> *First Presbyterian Church*
> *Santa Barbara, California*

ONE REMARRIED PARENT HOSTS

When the bride's remarried mother is the host. (This is an example without the year.)

> *Mr. and Mrs. John Sutton*
> *request the honour of your presence*
> *at the marriage of her daughter*
> *Susan Claire Craven*
> *to*
> *Mr. James Scott Newman*
> *Saturday, the sixth of June*
> *at four o'clock*
> *First Presbyterian Church*
> *Santa Barbara, California*

When the bride's remarried father hosts, it would read:

> *Mr. and Mrs. George Alan Craven*
> *request the honour of your presence*
> *at the marriage of his daughter*

A STEPMOTHER HOSTS

When the bride's stepmother and father sponsor the wedding the invitation can read as follows. This example would most commonly be used only if the stepmother raised the bride, or the bride's mother is deceased.

> *Mr. and Mrs. George Alan Craven*
> *request the honour of your presence*
> *at the marriage of Mrs. Craven's step-daughter*
> *Susan Claire*
> *to*
> *Mr. James Scott Newman*
> *Saturday, the sixth of June*
> *at four o'clock*
> *First Presbyterian Church*
> *Santa Barbara, California*

Another option, depending on their relationship is:

> *Mr. and Mrs. George Alan Craven*
> *request the honour of your presence*
> *at the marriage of their daughter*

DIVORCED UNMARRIED PARENTS CO-HOST

If the bride's parents are divorced and neither has remarried, the invitation may read:

> *Mrs. Lillian Jones Craven*
> *and*
> *Mr. George Alan Craven*
> *request the honour of your presence*
> *at the marriage of their daughter*
> *Susan Claire*
> *to*
> *Mr. James Scott Newman*
> *Saturday, the sixth of June*
> *at four o'clock*
> *First Presbyterian Church*
> *Santa Barbara, California*

BRIDE'S AND GROOM'S PARENTS CO-HOST

> *Mr. and Mrs. George Alan Craven*
> *and*
> *Mr. and Mrs. Michael Newman*
> *request the honour of your presence*
> *at the marriage of their children*
> *Susan Claire Craven*
> *and*
> *James Scott Newman*
> *Saturday, the sixth of June*
> *at four o'clock*
> *First Presbyterian Church*
> *Santa Barbara, California*

GROOM'S PARENTS HOST

When the groom's family sponsors the wedding, the invitation may read:

> *Mr. and Mrs. Michael Newman*
> *request the honour of your presence*
> *at the marriage of*
> *Susan Claire Craven*
> *to their son*
> *James Scott Newman*
> *Saturday, the sixth of June*
> *at four o'clock*
> *First Presbyterian Church*
> *Santa Barbara, California*

BRIDE AND GROOM HOST

When the bride and groom are sponsoring their own wedding, the traditional wording would be:

> *The honour of your presence*
> *is requested at the marriage of*
> *Susan Claire Craven*
> *to*
> *James Scott Newman*
> *Saturday, the sixth of June*
> *at four o'clock*
> *First Presbyterian Church*
> *Santa Barbara, California*

CONTEMPORARY WORDING

The following are examples of some contemporary wording:

BRIDE'S PARENTS HOST

A less formal invitation sponsored by the bride's parents.

> *We ask only those dearest in our hearts*
> *to join us in celebrating the marriage*
> *of our daughter Susan to James Scott Newman*
> *at four o'clock*
> *June sixth nineteen ninety-eight*
> *First Presbyterian Church*
> *Santa Barbara, California*
> *Lillian and George Craven*

BRIDE AND GROOM HOST

> *We invite you to join us*
> *in celebrating our love .*
> *On this day we will marry the one*
> *we laugh with, live for, dream with, love.*
> *We have chosen to continue our growth*
> *through marriage, please join*
> *Susan Claire*
> *and James Scott Newman*
> *at four o'clock*
> *Saturday, the sixth of June*
> *First Presbyterian Church*
> *Santa Barbara, California*

RECEPTION CARDS

One invitation will serve the purpose when all the guests are invited to both the ceremony and reception. However, when the ceremony and the reception are held in separate locations, you may enclose a reception card. Or when only a select number of guests are invited to the reception, a separate card is enclosed. It should be of the same paper and type style and is generally half the size. You may want to include directions or a map on the back. The following are examples of how the cards may read:

INFORMAL RECEPTION CARD

A less formal reception card would read:

> *Reception*
> *immediately following the ceremony*
> *Biltmore Hotel*
> *13495 Cabrillo Blvd.*
> *Santa Barbara*

FORMAL RECEPTION CARD

A formal reception card to accompany a formal invitation.

> *Mr. and Mrs. George Alan Craven*
> *request the pleasure of your company*
> *Saturday, the sixth of June*
> *at half past four o'clock*
> *Biltmore Hotel*
>
> *R.S.V.P.*
> *1523 Constance Way*
> *Santa Barbara, California*

INVITATION TO THE RECEPTION

If the ceremony is small or just for family members, but the reception guest list is larger, invitations are issued to the reception with ceremony cards enclosed. The invitation would read:

> *Mr. and Mrs. George Alan Craven*
> *request the pleasure of your company*
> *at the wedding reception of their daughter*
> *Susan Claire*
> *and*
> *Mr. James Scott Newman*
> *Saturday, the sixth of June*
> *at half after four o'clock*
> *Biltmore Hotel*
> *Santa Barbara, California*
> *Please respond*
> *1523 Constance Way*
> *Santa Barbara, California*

FORMAL CEREMONY CARD

Mr. and Mrs. George Alan Craven
request the honour of your presence
Saturday, the sixth of June
at four o'clock
First Presbyterian Church
Santa Barbara, California

INFORMAL CEREMONY CARD

Ceremony
at Four o'clock
First Presbyterian Church

TRADITIONAL ANNOUNCEMENT

Mr. and Mrs. George Alan Craven
have the honour of announcing
the marriage of their daughter
Susan Claire
and
Mr. James Scott Newman
on Saturday, the sixth of June
Nineteen hundred and ninety-eight
Santa Barbara, California

RESPONSE CARD

When a response card is sent out, it should be accompanied by a self addressed, pre-stamped envelope. The following are some examples.

The favour of a reply is requested
by the twenty-first day of May
M _____
will _____ *attend*

or

Please respond on or before
the twenty-first of May
M _____
will _____ *attend*

TRADITIONAL PEW CARD

Catherine and Robert
First Presbyterian Church
Bride's Section
Pew Number _____

or

M _____
First Presbyterian Church
Bride's Section
Pew Number _____

If your taste runs to the romantic, you may wish to replace the standard wording with sentiments that better reflect your feelings. Tread carefully here, and try to maintain a light touch. You want to be very sure you're comfortable with the wording before your invitations are printed. Peruse sample invitation books, wedding books, and bridal magazines to cull ideas for alternative wording. When in doubt, opt for simplicity. When you compose the ceremony, you and your fiancé will get another chance to express your feelings about the day and your future life together.

I'd like to briefly mention one item that definitely does not belong on your invitation: the name of your gift registry. This information should be disseminated by you, your close friends, or your relatives. It's inappropriate to mention gifts when you're asking someone to attend your wedding. Naturally, this rule also applies to requests for money instead of gifts.

INVITATION KEEPSAKES

Among all the photographs and memorabilia that document your wedding, the invitation holds a very special place. Many brides find innovative ways to preserve the card itself or the wording alone. Though mounting the invitation in a narrow gold frame is the traditional choice, your own personal style can lead you to other options.

Have your invitation mounted in a shadowbox, along with some dried blossoms from your wedding bouquet. The box can be set on a table or hung on a wall in your new home.

Have the wording of your invitation embroidered or written with fabric paint on a small pillow.

Engrave the wording of your invitation on a

ABOVE: *WEDDING INVITATION AND HAND-CALLIGRAPHIED MARRIAGE CERTIFICATE CUSTOM FRAMED: YESTERYEAR. STYLED: SUNDAY HENDRICKSON. PHOTO: MICHAEL GARLAND*
OPPOSITE: *EXQUISITE TABLE SETTING FEATURES BEAUTIFULLY DESIGNED MENU CARD, COORDINATING GOLD OVAL-FRAMED PHOTO PLACECARD FAVORS AND GOLD STAR-COVERED CHOCOLATE TRUFFLE BOXES, TIED WITH GOLD MESH, FRENCH WIRED RIBBON. PHOTO: G. GREGORY GEIGER*

beautiful crystal or silver box or bowl. Either of these can be filled with potpourri or candy and displayed on a table in the living room of your new home.

Hand-paint or silk-screen the wording of your invitation on a porcelain plate. The plate can be displayed in a china cabinet or hung on a wall.

Find an artist who can paint or otherwise decorate your invitation, then frame and display it. A stationer might refer you to an artist who specializes in keepsake invitations.

WEDDING STATIONERY

While you're ordering your invitations, you might also consider the other wedding-related stationery you'll need. It's extremely useful, as well as cost-effective, to have everything printed at the same time. The most frequently used wedding-stationery items are announcements, thank-you cards, and at-home cards.

Announcements are sent to acquaintances, business associates, or to those whom you know will not be able to attend the ceremony. An

announcement does not require a gift, so it's a nice way to inform people of your marriage without obligating them. Announcements may be sent by either set of parents, by both sets, or by the couple themselves. They are mailed the day of the ceremony or the day after. The wedding date is included, but not the time or location of the ceremony and reception.

For thank-you notes, you may choose a folded card with your name or monogram imprinted on the outside, a folded piece of stationery, or cards printed with the words

ABOVE: *A distinguished bridal table placecard and heart-shaped box, sculpted of sugar-based pastalage, by Jan Kish, make splendid keepsakes. White chocolate tiny basket filled with chocolate truffles by Lee Gelfond Chocolates, also makes delicious favors. Invitations shown by Margaret Di Piazza and Anna Griffin.*

BELOW: *Delightful selection of decorated candies and monogrammed mints created by Jan Kish. Styling: Sunday Hendrickson. Photos: Michael Garland.*

ABOVE: *White satin moire, graced with an elegant ribbon rose guest book from Beverly Clark Collection.*
PHOTO: HENRY HAMAMOTO. BELOW: PHOTO: DURANGO STEELE

"Thank You." Make sure to order enough—extras can always be used later. If possible, send a thank-you note as soon as you have received a gift. Sign your maiden name or first name before the wedding and your married name afterward. It's always best to mention the gift; it sounds more personal, except in the case of a gift of money. When thanking someone for money, never mention the amount. It's a nice touch, though, to tell them what you intend to purchase with their gift.

At-home cards inform your friends of your new address and let them know whether you're keeping your maiden name.

They are usually included with the announcement or sent separately after the wedding.

There is another category of cards you should purchase when you're ordering your stationery. These include the smaller items used at the reception: table numbers, name cards, and menu cards. You will hand-print the information on the table-number and name cards when the details of the wedding have been established.

You can also purchase a guest book and pen at your stationer's or at a bridal salon, but these might be good items to register for as shower gifts.

TYPE DESIGN AND PRINTING

In medieval times, wealthy families hired monks to hand-pen their wedding invitations in the same ornate calligraphy the monks used for illustrated manuscripts. An invitation was a true work of art and symbolized the family's status. When the printing press was invented, the first typefaces were designed to look like the monks' fine penmanship. The descendants of those classic fonts are still used today for formal wedding invitations.

Invitations for more casual weddings may bear any typeface you desire, as long as it is in keeping with the spirit of your wedding. Typefaces have definite personalities, as you'll discover the moment you begin to look through sample books at the stationer's. You'll either order your invitations from these books, or use them as inspiration for a custom design. If you have a very healthy budget, a graphic designer can create a unique invitation based on your suggestions or on the style and theme of your wedding. Some people have an artist friend who'll agree to design the invitation as a wedding gift.

The majority of couples, though, will select their invitations from among the stationery store's samples. There you'll find a myriad of invitation designs, typefaces, and ink colors.

Calligraphy, a highly decorative form of penmanship, was at one time used primarily to address envelopes. It has become increasingly popular over the last few years, due not only to the resurgence of formal weddings but also to the availability of new, computerized inscribing machines that create a flawless script that looks handcrafted. These machines are not laser printers but instead use a calligraphy pen that is computer driven. Although most machines can inscribe only one or two invitations at a time, it's faster and less expensive than having the invitations hand-penned by a calligrapher (still another option, of course).

ABOVE AND BELOW: *Custom designed invitations: Ann Fiedler Creations. Picture frame favor by Keepsakes. Floral bouquet: Hearts Bloom*

THE COMPLETE INVITATION

The simplest wedding invitation may be a handwritten message on an elegant note card; for a small wedding, such a personal touch might strike just the right chord. Most couples, however, find themselves at the stationer's faced with a baffling series of decisions regarding enclosures, response cards, announcements, and more.

The wedding invitation itself is usually the largest item in the ensemble. If the ceremony and reception are held at the same location, a separate reception card is not required. If they are to be held at different sites, a smaller reception card should be enclosed. A reception card is also used if only a select number of guests are to be invited to the reception. Sometimes the reception is the larger of the two events, in which case the sizes of the cards are reversed: the reception card is large, and a small ceremony card is included for the group invited to witness the vows.

You may also want to include a directions card, if the location is difficult to find or if many of the guests will be from out of town. In a formal invitation, all of these are enclosed in both an inner and an outer envelope. The outer envelope will be printed with the return address of whoever is handling the guest list—usually the bride or her mother.

Many invitations now include response cards with addressed, stamped envelopes. Long frowned upon by etiquette experts, response cards take the place of *RSVP* at the bottom of the invitation. The reason for the growing popularity of these cards is simple: good manners have fallen upon hard times, and some people won't respond at all unless they are given a card to fill out and the stamped envelope in which to mail it. I recommend response cards because they make your life easier. Even if you enclose them, you'll most likely have to phone one or two guests during the final week to find out whether they'll be attending.

TOP ROW *LEFT TO RIGHT:*

ROSE PRINT CARDS: CLAUDIA LAUB STUDIO

GOLD-TIED: ANN FIEDLER CREATIONS

GOLD HEART: LA VIE EN ROSE

GOLD CHERUB: ANNA GRIFFIN

IVORY SATIN BOW: ANN FIEDLER CREATIONS

BOTTOM ROW *LEFT TO RIGHT:*

FLOWER CONE: MARGARET DI PIAZZA

ROSE TOPIARY: KEEPSAKES

HEART PROGRAM: LA VIE EN ROSE

GOLD AND IVORY BOW: ANNA GRIFFIN

HAND-WRAPPED: MARGARET DI PIAZZA

PLACE CARD: ANN FIEDLER CREATIONS

CHERUB DECORATED BOX: KEEPSAKES

ABOVE: *A SELECTION OF ELABORATELY ETCHED SILVER PLATED PENS FROM BEVERLY CLARK COLLECTION.* OPPOSITE: *HANDMADE PAPER INVITATION WITH SATIN BOWS: BARBARA LOGAN. EMBOSSED CHERUB INVITATION AND MATCHING PLACECARDS: ANN FIEDLER. WHITE CHOCOLATE BRIDE SCULPTURE: LEE GELFOND CHOCOLATES. SMALL CONES, FILLED WITH ROSE PETALS, TIED WITH ORGANZA BOWS: WRAPPINGS. STYLING: SUNDAY HENDRICKSON PHOTO: MICHAEL GARLAND.*

If yours is to be a large wedding, you may wish to include a pew card. Pew cards are used to invite special guests or close relatives to be seated toward the front, in a reserved section designated by ribbons. The pew card may be handwritten or engraved. It is mailed after the guest has accepted the wedding invitation: those holding pew cards should hand them to the usher before being seated.

Some people are mystified by the little sheets of tissue paper slipped inside formal wedding invitations. These are a holdover from the days when such tissues were used to blot ink that might still be damp. They are purely for show now, but many brides include them because of the elegant impression they make.

A STATIONERY OVERVIEW

At-home cards. These cards inform friends of your new address.

Ceremony cards. This card is enclosed when a select few guests are invited to the ceremony and to the reception, to which all guests are invited.

Ceremony program. A program stating the order in which events will take place during the ceremony. It will list songs, prayers, and scriptures to be read as well as unusual customs, along with names of the attendants, vocalist, and musicians.

Invitations. Order a few more than you think you'll need.

Maps. Small maps printed with directions to the ceremony and/or reception site.

Pew cards. Used in large, formal weddings, they indicate special seating positions.

Rain cards. These inform guests, invited to an outdoor wedding, of an alternative location in case of rain.

Reception cards. Used when only a select number of the guests invited to the ceremony are also invited to the reception.

Response cards. Guests return this card to inform the hosts of whether or not they will be attending the wedding.

Thank-you cards. Small cards, usually folded, used to express your thanks for gifts received.

Travel cards. These inform guests of any special wedding day transportation you have arranged, such as a bus or trolley to take out-of-town guests from their hotel to the ceremony. The card can also be used to indicate parking locations and tell guests whether fees or gratuities have been paid in advance.

Weekend wedding program. Informs guests of the activities scheduled for the weekend and of suggested attire. Includes information on travel or lodging arrangements you have made.

ORDERING YOUR INVITATIONS AND STATIONERY

Shop around a bit to get ideas before choosing a stationer. Select a stationer who offers a wide variety of styles and price ranges, is knowledgeable about wording and typefaces, and is open to your questions and suggestions.

When ordering invitations, figure on one for each couple, one for each single person, and another for his or her date, if dates are to be invited. A separate invitation should also be sent to children who are sixteen or older. Remember to order invitations for the officiant, attendants, their dates (if invited), and both sets of parents. Order several extra invitations for keepsakes, mistakes, and last-minute invitees.

Proofread your invitations and other stationery carefully, both when you place the order and when you pick up the finished pieces. If possible check the wording and layout after the typesetting has been done but before the invitation is printed. Take someone along to help you proofread.

ADDRESSING AND MAILING

There used to be only one acceptable way to address wedding invitations: by hand. Nowadays, the inscribing machines mentioned earlier offer a perfectly fine alternative. Though these machines save time and produce a perfect script, don't disregard the charm of hand-addressed envelopes.

Hiring a calligrapher is another option, but they can be costly. One resourceful bride I know turned to the art department of a local university for a calligrapher. A notice on the department bulletin board put her in touch with a talented student who did the work beautifully for a reasonable rate.

The names, address, and zip code should appear on the outside envelope. If your invitation includes an inside envelope, repeat the names there and add the first names of any children who are invited. Children over sixteen should receive their own invitation. For a single person, write the name and the words "and guest" (if invited) on the inside envelope; if you know the guest's name, a separate invitation should be sent. When two people live together, send one invitation addressed to both. Formal titles such as Doctor, Captain, and Reverend should be written out, while Ms., Mrs., and Mr. may be abbreviated.

ABOVE: *Silver tray displays an array of favors by Keepsakes, each embellished with tulle ribbons and roses.*
BELOW: *Decorative frosting enhances bell-shaped cookies and almond favors. A few of the incredible candy treats created by*
Jan Kish. OPPOSITE: *Exquisitely crafted, handmade paper cones, hand calligraphied and gold-sealed are filled with flowers to toss*
at the bride and groom as they depart. Designed by Margaret Di Piazza. Flowers: Hearts Bloom

The invitation should be placed in the envelope with the engraved side facing up. Extra enclosures such as pew cards, reception cards, or at-home cards may be placed next to the engraved side or inserted in the fold, if any. The unsealed inner envelope is then placed in the outer envelope so that the guests' names are seen first when the envelope is opened. Weigh the invitation before mailing to ensure proper postage. Stamps featuring flowers, fruit, cupids, or the ever-popular "love" design reflect the spirit of the invitation inside.

FAVORS

Just as invitations have become more imaginative over the past few years, wedding favors, too, have become more creative. The first wedding favors

were gifts of food: the bride and groom would present their departing guests with spice buns, fruits, or nuts. Sugar-coated almonds are still widely chosen as wedding favors, a custom begun by the Italians, for whom the almonds symbolize the bitterness and sweetness of married life.

In England's Elizabethan era, "tying the knot" was transformed from a literal description into a fashionable wedding favor. Early Northern European cultures had celebrated marriage by binding the bride and groom together with ropes around their waists on their wedding day. The romantic Elizabethans took this ancient custom and refined it, using brightly colored, knotted ribbons to decorate their wedding attire. Both men and women adorned themselves with these ribbons, which they called favors. Royalty used silver or gold ribbons, while everyone else used white and blue. At the ceremony, guests would be presented with small bouquets of flowers tied with the ribbons, and these, too, were called favors.

For wealthy noblemen, simple nosegays with knotted ribbons were not considered an adequate tribute. Favors at their weddings were more extravagant: jewelry, scarves, gloves, or handkerchiefs. The latter were often stitched with the initials of the bride and groom. These were perhaps forerunners of today's monogrammed napkins and matchbooks.

The Elizabethan sense of romance is reflected in the favors given today. Although a simple, tulle-wrapped handful of Jordan almonds is always appropriate, brides and wedding designers have focused on the humble favor as an outlet for their creativity. Almonds are still

used, and are placed in miniature, hand-painted flower pots or delicate baskets. Even tulle has gone glamorous, twinkling with stars, sparkles, or pearls.

Silver frames wrapped in tulle and decorated with silk blossoms make a delightful wedding favor. Keepsakes, a company in Southern California, designs such frames to match a wedding's style and color scheme. Margaret DiPiazza, of New York City, specializes in creating monogrammed paper cones that can be filled with petals for tossing over the bride and groom. Shown left, each cone is hand-printed in gold ink, in Margaret's graceful calligraphy. Jan Kish, of Worthington, Ohio, makes mints that are monogrammed in gold or white chocolate. These elegant confections, presented in a keepsake porcelain bowl or gold-leafed box, taste as good as they look. Lee Gelfond, of Beverly Hills, has earned a reputation for creating innovative chocolate wedding favors: chocolate baskets filled with truffles, chocolate swans filled with sweets, and other whimsical treats.

Browse wedding books and magazines for inspiration, or ask your florist to suggest some ideas. Friends may recall appealing favors from weddings they've attended. Though they are a relatively minor detail in your wedding picture, innovative favors leave a lasting impression on your guests.

CELEBRATIONS

OVER THE CENTURIES couples have married for power, for wealth, to honor an arrangement made at their birth, and—most commonly, for love. Whatever the reason for a marriage, one element has remained constant: weddings have always inspired celebrations.

Today, there are parties that celebrate every step to the altar—engagement parties, bridal showers, bachelor and bachelorette dinners, rehearsal dinners, luncheons, and brunches. Depending on your family and circle of friends, the revelry can last for months. In the nineteenth century, weddings were often celebrated for at least a week, especially if they took place in the countryside, with guests traveling many miles to attend. Multiple parties were appropriate then, and they still are today.

ENGAGEMENT PARTIES

Engagement parties used to be more commonplace than they are today. With the rising cost of weddings, many couples prefer to save all their funds for the reception rather than host an engagement party. It's not necessary for the couple or their parents to host the party, however, friends can sponsor one, too.

Engagement parties often serve a practical purpose. If the couple will be married out of town, their friends can host an engagement party and celebrate the happy occasion even if they cannot attend the wedding itself. Similarly, if the wedding will be small, an engagement party gives a larger gathering of friends and family the chance to toast to the couple's health and happiness.

Few rules apply to engagement parties. They may be as casual or as formal as the host likes.

ABOVE: *An engagement cake for two, with knotted gold cord signifies "tying the knot." Photo and styling: Sunday Hendrickson. Cake: Patticakes* PREVIOUS PAGE: *Pillared terrace provides the perfect garden setting for an outdoor bridal shower. Flowers by Fleurs. Photo: G. Gregory Geiger. Elegant silver teapot table arrangement by Hearts Bloom. Photo: Jennifer Drake.* RIGHT: *Sponged gold terra-cotta flower pot bears the name of the bride and groom. Flowers: Laurels Custom Florist. Photo: Amedeo*

Much of that spirit is returning again today. Once more, family and friends often trek long distances to share in the event, inspiring more couples to turn the wedding day into a wedding weekend or week. In the months before the wedding, your friends and relatives will want to celebrate by honoring you with dinners and parties. Certainly, you should enjoy all the attention, but try not to have too many activities scheduled very close to the wedding date, since you will likely need time to attend to last-minute details.

ABOVE AND RIGHT: *Designed by Scott Hogue, this unique combination arrangement includes luscious fruit, festive flowers and even delicate feathers to make a dramatic centerpiece for an engagement dinner. Photo: Jacky Winter*
BELOW: *Platter of glorious grapes.*
Photo: Durango Steele

BRIDAL SHOWERS

The first bridal shower was inspired by an age-old situation: two people fall madly in love but are nearly foiled by a disapproving father. Legend has it that the father of a certain young lady forbade her to marry a poor Dutch miller and refused to provide her with a dowry. The miller's friends came to the rescue by showering the bride with all the household items she would need to start a new life with her husband. Thus began the tradition of presenting the bride with gifts, both practical and purely romantic, to help her feather the nest.

Bridal showers today are a source of great merriment for all involved. What can be more delightful than unwrapping scads of presents, with no stressful ceremony and reception to worry about? Showers also give your friends and family a chance to get to know one another before the wedding. Like weddings, showers can be informal affairs or very proper luncheons. Once a ladies-only event, the wedding shower may now include the men as well. Coed showers are particularly popular with older couples, who are likely to have a

ABOVE AND OPPOSITE: *Exquisite centerpieces with lilacs, roses and dendrobium orchids, are ideal for a bridal shower. Flowers: Laurels Custom Florist Photos: Amedeo, courtesy of* Flowers& *magazine* BELOW: *Delightful bridal shower cake, bears the message "Showers of Love" Cake: Patticakes.*

number of married friends.

Showers are usually given a month or two before the wedding. It's customary for a close friend, the maid of honor, a relative, or a bridesmaid to give the shower. It is generally not hosted by your mother or immediate family, although they may help. Today it's common for two or more people to host a shower together to ease the financial burden. Sometimes several people from different areas of your life—work colleagues, college pals, hometown friends—will offer to give you a shower. If you are given more than one, try not to invite the same people to every shower. Weddings can become expensive for guests, especially for your bridal party, so don't take the joy out of it for them by overtaxing their gift budgets.

The traditional all-female shower is an afternoon luncheon or tea for ten to twenty guests. Invitations are usually sent, but this is not mandatory. Generally, the hostess and the bride get together to determine a date, a guest list, and the style, formality, and theme of the shower. Sometimes, the hostess may surprise the bride and get the information from her fiancé.

Not everyone who is invited to the wedding need be invited to the shower. Guests are usually close friends or relatives, or perhaps you may have one shower with each group. Avoid any hurt feelings by only inviting people to the shower who are invited to the reception, unless the wedding is taking place out of town or will include only close family members.

With all the excitement and opening of gifts at a bridal shower, it's easy to misplace the cards and lose track of who gave what. To avoid confusion, have someone keep a list of each gift as it's opened. Show your appreciation by sending a thank-you note within a week of the shower. If you wait longer, this essential courtesy may be forgotten amid the hectic pre-wedding plans.

ABOVE: *Heart-shaped lace-trimmed form conveniently creates the traditional shower gift ribbon bouquet which can be carried at the wedding rehearsal. Beverly Clark Collection.* RIGHT TOP AND BOTTOM: *Bridal shower hosted by Marcia Valentino for her future daughter-in-law, Angelique, held at the Four Seasons Biltmore.* CENTER: *Shower gifts. Photos: Durango Steele*

OPPOSITE: *Individual tea cup floral arrangements designed by Hearts Bloom graced tables filled with delicacies from Montecito Confectioners in the lovely garden setting. Photo: Jennifer Drake*

CLAUDIA KUNIN

Showers with a Theme

Not so long ago, most newlyweds were young and inexperienced in the art of furnishing a home. This is less the case today. Many couples have been out on their own for some time before they marry and have already accumulated many household items. A theme shower affords such couples the opportunity to fine-tune their wish list and have a lot of fun as well. Theme showers are also a smart idea if the couple will be given more than one shower: having two different themes will help prevent duplicate gifts. Some popular themes:

Lingerie showers are a favorite, perhaps because so many working women rarely allow themselves to indulge in clothes that are "impractical" and unabashedly romantic. Lacy nightgowns, delicate camisoles, silk teddies, sexy bras, or a sleek satin robe are sure to make the bride's honeymoon a little sweeter. Other thoughtful gifts might be perfume, bath accessories, or jewelry. Or, get a baby picture of the bride's fiancé from his mother and put it in a pretty frame. The bride will cherish it throughout the years to come.

Linen showers are a savvy choice. Here, at last, is your chance to get those 300-thread-count cotton sheets you've lusted after for years. Though you might have a number of linens already, these will eventually wear out. Taking a fresh, brand-new set of towels from the box three years from now will be a real treat. If you decide on a linen shower, you might want to let everyone know your color scheme. It can be helpful to register in a department store for items such as monogrammed towels, a scale, bathroom sets and accessories, bed sheets, pillows, or blankets.

Kitchen showers are an especially good theme for coed parties. Gift ideas are endless, ranging from inexpensive kitchen tools to more costly appliances such as automatic bread makers or food processors. Browse through a specialty kitchen shop or department store to view the possibilities, and if you have definite items in mind, register for them. One fun idea is to have each guest bring a favorite recipe along with one item needed for its preparation: chocolate chip cookies with the cookie sheets, quiche lorraine with a quiche dish. The hostess may provide a recipe box to put the recipes in, or she could put them in a special notebook that will preserve the memories of the day.

Bridesmaids' Party

Your bridesmaids deserve a special party all their own. Throughout the pre-wedding months, they will most likely entertain you and provide tremendous help with planning and shopping. A splendid luncheon, an afternoon tea, or an elegant dinner party that includes spouses and dates will let them know how much you appreciate their efforts.

The bridesmaids' party usually takes place a day or so before the wedding, when all the attendants have arrived in town. This little celebration gives them an opportunity to get to know one another and to go over last-minute plans with you. You can also give them their gifts at this time.

Some brides prefer an outing to a bridesmaids' luncheon. You might like to treat your bridesmaids to a day at a nearby health spa, complete with massage and facial. If you live near a body of water, an afternoon cruise might be a relaxing prelude to the hectic days ahead. Perhaps a luncheon in a picturesque part of town, followed by a few hours of shopping or sightseeing, would have the most appeal. Try to choose something everyone will enjoy, and, if at all possible, keep the pace leisurely. This may be your last chance as a single woman to chat and reminisce with these close friends.

LEFT AND OPPOSITE: *Bridesmaid's luncheon two tier cake is resplendently accented with fresh flowers.*
Cakes: Patticake. Flowers: The Flower Studio. Styled by: Sunday Hendrickson. Photo: Claudia Kunin, courtesy of
Romantic Homes magazine. ABOVE: *wedding attendants pose in a white gazebo. Photo: Joshua Ets-Hokin*

BACHELOR PARTIES

The bachelor party is by nature bittersweet. It's the groom's last night out with the boys as a single man. The party may be planned by the best man and the ushers or hosted by the groom himself. The evening is usually a long one and the wine flows plentifully, so it's not a bad idea to see to it that the party takes place a few days or a week before the wedding. Traditionally, the festivities begin with a dinner where the groom makes a champagne toast to his bride. In days past, each man would smash his glass after the toast so that it would never be used for a less worthy purpose. The tradition is rarely carried to

this extreme anymore, but the chivalrous groom will still toast his bride.

Occasionally, a bride will feel uncomfortable about the bachelor party. In these cases, I might advise her to keep her reservations to herself and maintain a sense of humor. At this point, so close to the wedding day, her nerves are apt to be quite jangled. It would be a shame to let her discomfort hamper her groom's good time. Besides, the bachelor party isn't simply an excuse for a wild night on the town. The groom may also want to give his attendants their gifts or review their duties and make last-minute plans.

TOP: *IMAGINATIVE BACHELOR PARTY INVITATIONS DESIGNED BY LA VIE EN ROSE. PHOTO: MICHAEL GARLAND. STYLED BY: SUNDAY HENDRICKSON*
BOTTOM LEFT AND RIGHT: *A DASH OF IMAGINATION PHOTOS: DURANGO STEELE*
BOTTOM CENTER: *HANDSOME PARTY OF THE GROOM AND HIS GROOMSMEN. PHOTO: FRED MARCUS PHOTOGRAPHY*

WELCOMING OUT-OF-TOWN GUESTS

Most couples will play host to family and friends from out of town. While you're planning your parties and outings, keep a separate checklist for these guests. The list should include information about their arrival times, transportation, accommodations, and perhaps the name of an "escort." The escort is a person assigned to each visiting family who can answer questions and make sure they're happy and comfortable. If visitors don't have such an escort, the bride or groom will usually assume that role.

Before the wedding day, you'll certainly want to spend time with guests who've traveled all those miles to join you. In the weeks before the wedding, show your appreciation with a little extra hospitality: offer to arrange accommodations at the home of a relative or friend, or provide them with the names of hotels or inns you think they'd enjoy. If your guests arrive a day or two before the wedding, you may arrange for a basket of fruit or flowers to greet them in their hotel room, or plan a special luncheon, or invite them to the rehearsal dinner.

ABOVE: *Hanging baskets of colorful flowers.*

PHOTO: *G. Gregory Geiger*

BELOW: *Afternoon tea welcomes guests!*

PHOTO: *Jennifer Drake*

The Rehearsal Dinner

In recent years, the rehearsal dinner has become a highlight of the wedding celebration. This is the time when the attendants and other close friends can mingle with the bride and groom and their immediate families in a convivial, intimate setting. The dinner, which usually takes place immediately following the rehearsal, is a wonderful opportunity to thank the wedding party again for their help throughout the long months of planning.

The groom's parents usually host the dinner, but this is not a rigid rule. Anyone, or any combination of people can host the occasion. If the groom's parents want to fund the event but would rather not plan it, you might persuade a friend or relative to help you organize the party.

It is customary for the guests to include both sets of parents, all the adult attendants of the bridal party with their spouses or dates, and the parents of the child attendants. Small children should be taken home after the rehearsal to get a good night's sleep so they will be on their best behavior for the wedding. You may also want to include other relatives and out-of-town guests.

If the party takes place the night before the ceremony, make it an early evening and encourage only moderate drinking. You'll surely want everyone to feel their best the next day. The gracious bride will toast both her parents and thank her bridal party. If you haven't already done so, you may give them their gifts at this time.

Floral designer Scott Hogue created a colorful Mexican fiesta for this rehearsal dinner, complete with sarapes, streamers and piñatas. Brightly decorated straw sombreros add pizazz to the table decor. Mariachis serenade guests at the El Paseo Restaurant, Santa Barbara, CA.
Photos: Clint Weisman

101

WEDDING-DAY AND DAY-AFTER PARTIES

Hosting a light breakfast or early lunch on the day of the wedding is an ideal way for a friend or relative to participate in the wedding festivities. The bride and groom and their families are not expected to attend these parties, although they may certainly do so if they like. If the wedding is late in the afternoon or evening, a brunch or luncheon will entertain your out-of-town guests while you take care of last-minute preparations. If your wedding will take place in the morning, a dinner party that evening would be nice to organize for your out-of-town guests. It needn't be formal at all, simply an invitation to continue the merrymaking. Otherwise, your guests might end up languishing in their hotel rooms while you're happily on the way to your honeymoon destination.

Many couples arrange a brunch or luncheon for their out-of-town guests the day after the wedding. In fact, this has become a popular feature of weddings at which more than a few of the guests hail from faraway places. There are several ways to go about it: the bride and groom may treat everyone; a relative may offer to host; or the bride and groom may arrange the event and ask that each guest pay a set fee.

The day-after party is generally a relaxed but high-spirited affair, especially if the bride and groom postpone their honeymoon for a day in order to join in the fun. Many newlyweds wouldn't dream of missing a chance to relive the wedding highlights, detail their vacation plans, and simply bask in the afterglow of the big event. Even if the bride and groom are not able to attend, the brunch is a generous finishing touch to the wedding celebration.

THIS PAGE: *For out-of-town guests, a special day-after wedding brunch was created by floral designer Scott Hogue, in an outdoor garden theme. Potted plants frame the entrance to the patio of the Santa Barbara Music Academy where tables are topped with burlap table squares, tall topiaries, pots of tulips and miniature roses. Napkins are tied with raffia, adding the final touch. Photo: Clint Weisman*

OPPOSITE: *Scott Hogue created an imaginative centerpiece using grapes, artichokes and flowers. Photo: Jacky Winter*

THE WEDDING PARTY

Your WEDDING DAY may be the closest you ever come to starring in an elaborate production. Like any leading lady, you'll depend on your supporting players for encouragement and inspiration. Your wedding party will be a source of comfort, ideas, and advice as you carefully construct the details of your perfect day. Each member has a slightly different role to play, depending on custom and on individual personalities. One bridesmaid might be just right for your treks to bridal salons. Another might help create favors for the place settings. Don't overlook your parents. With all the tasks involved in preparation, there's room for everyone to lend a hand. Each member of the wedding party will feel more important if you ask or assign each a specific task in either your ceremony or your reception.

STEPHANIE HOGUE

THE PARENTS

Your parents will most likely take a keen interest in all the wedding preparations. If your mom lives in the same town as you do, she will certainly want to savor every moment of these few whirlwind months. Even if she resides some distance away, she can help with advice and decisions. In addition to assisting you with the guest list and keeping your father apprised of the proceedings, your mother will play a key part on the day of the wedding. She is the last person seated at the ceremony, the first to greet the guests in the receiving line and the official hostess at the reception. Your parents will sit at a place of honor at the reception—either at the head table with the bride, groom, and groom's parents, or at a table with other family members.

Many a proud father attests that escorting his beloved daughter down the aisle was one of the highlights of his life. Although acceptable today,

some brides prefer to walk alone. You may want to think twice before making this decision or you may want to include both parents.

After the ceremony, your father may either stand in the receiving line or mingle with the guests. He'll be the last person to leave the reception, after settling the bill with the caterer, musicians, and other vendors.

The degree to which the groom's parents are involved in the wedding depends on your desires, their financial contribution, and their proximity to the wedding location. It is customary for the groom's parents to send a note or phone the bride and her parents, welcoming her into their family. Their largest role in the festivities usually comes in hosting the rehearsal dinner party. After the ceremony, the groom's mother stands in the receiving line; the father may or may not. The groom's parents may be seated at the head table with the bride and groom or separately with his family members.

STEPHANIE HOGUE

ABOVE: *WIDE-BRIMMED SUMMER HATS, TRIMMED WITH DELICATE PINK ROSES ADD AN ENGAGING TOUCH TO THESE BRIDESMAIDS, DRESSED IN WHITE TEA-LENGTH DRESSES, AND USHERS IN WHITE DINNER JACKETS. THE HANDSOME GROUP COMPLEMENT THE BRIDE'S ELEGANT OFF-THE-SHOULDER SATIN AND LACE GOWN, CREATING A PICTURE-PERFECT WEDDING PARTY. PHOTO: CLAY BLACKMORE. BELOW: A ROMANTIC EMBRACE. PHOTO: DURANGO STEELE*

THE ATTENDANTS

For every bride and groom, there have always been bridesmaids and groomsmen, though their duties have changed dramatically. From ancient Rome through the Middle Ages, bridesmaids had two purposes: to protect the bride from evil spirits and the groomsmen, and to stand as witnesses for her. In those days, a woman was viewed as the property of her father, and was often married against her will. To curb this practice, societies required at least two witnesses who would attest to the bride's willingness, one of whom was her closest friend, her maid of honor.

Today's attendants still offer priceless support, but before asking everyone to become your "attendant", consider this: the more attendants you have, the more you'll need to spend on bouquets, boutonnieres, and gifts. Ask only friends and family members who are special to you and for whom being in your wedding will not be financially burdensome.

The Maid or Matron of Honor

Brides usually choose a maid or matron of honor with whom they feel especially close: a sister or a best friend. If you're having a large wedding you may want both a married sister or friend as the matron, and an unmarried woman as the maid of honor.

Your maid or matron of honor will be at your side throughout the planning stages as well as the ceremony. If she lives nearby, she can help with details such as addressing envelopes, making favors, and shopping for flowers and the myriad other items you'll need. She'll contact the bridesmaids about fittings and will shepherd them on the day of the wedding, when she'll help you with your dress as well. The maid or matron of honor often hosts a bridal shower, either by herself or with the bridesmaids. She is a member of the receiving line and is seated in a place of honor at the reception.

The bridal wardrobe. Photo: Durango Steele

Extensive bridal party, attending the Connie Goodman and David Litman wedding, formally poses for an impressive photograph. Bridesmaids wearing exquisitely designed champagne-colored gowns carry elaborate floral bouquets, inventively wrapped in matching fabric. Chuppah in the background is draped in tulle, sprinkled with stars of metallic gold. Floral designer: Barbara Taylor. Photo: Monte Clay

THE BEST MAN

The groom generally selects his brother, a close relative, or his best friend to be the best man, but he can also select his father or, in the case of a second marriage, his son. The best man not only offers moral support but is also the groom's right-hand man in organizing activities and handling important tasks. Some of these include coordinating the ushers' fittings and playing coach to them on the wedding day; holding the ring(s) until the appropriate moment in the ceremony; paying the clergy; and making the first toast to the newlyweds at the reception. One of his major duties is to see to it that the groom makes it through the day intact—the best man drives the groom to the ceremony, helps him dress, and makes sure that he has the plane tickets, traveler's checks, and suitcases secured in the honeymoon car.

ABOVE: *Brett Levkoff and his zealous ring bearer, Demetrious Elias, share a moment.*
Photo: Fred Marcus Photography. LEFT: *Even the groom gets involved in the last minute preparations.*
Photo: Durango Steele.

OPPOSITE TOP ROW: *Getting to the ceremony on time. Photo: Calvin Hayes. Bride and bridesmaids relax on the lawn. Photo: Durango Steele.* CENTER ROW: *A little advice for the groom. Photo: Durango Steele. Gondola carries the wedding party to a waterside reception. Photo: The Gondola Getaway. Ushers share a leisure moment. Photo: Durango Steele.*
BOTTOM ROW: *The ultimate photo opportunity! Photo: Brian Kramer. Groom and attendants ready to celebrate. Photo: Durango Steele*

ABOVE: *Groom and groomsmen pose together. Photo: Heidi Mauracher*

Groomsmen

As with the bridesmaids, you may have any number of groomsmen you desire, although the size of the wedding generally determines the number. A good rule to follow is one groomsman for every fifty guests. As noted, while you're not required to have the same number of groomsmen as bridesmaids, doing so makes for a better-balanced procession.

The groomsmen are usually brothers, relatives, or close friends of the bride or groom. On the day of the wedding, they'll arrive at the church one hour before the ceremony to begin seating the guests. They'll distribute wedding service programs, direct the placement of gifts, and escort the bridesmaids out of the church during the recessional.

BRIDESMAIDS

How many bridesmaids should you have? There are no hard-and-fast rules, although small weddings rarely have more than six. Large formal weddings usually have eight, and often up to twelve, bridesmaids. It's not necessary to have the same number of bridesmaids and grooms-men, but doing so provides a pleasing symmetry at the altar and in the wedding photos.

The bridesmaids are usually close friends or sisters of the bride or groom. Their duties are few, but they add a colorful touch to the wedding. Bridesmaids may give the bride a shower and help her with pre-wedding errands. They'll be invited to the pre-wedding parties, the rehearsal, and the rehearsal dinner.

ABOVE: *FUN-LOVING BRIDESMAIDS KICK OFF THEIR SHOES.*

LEFT: *CHECKING THOSE LAST MINUTE DETAILS.*

PHOTOS: *DURANGO STEELE*

ABOVE: *Adorable flower girl and her favorite dog.*
PHOTO: *Durango Steel.*
LEFT: *A touching moment with a faithful friend.*
PHOTO: *Clay Blackmore.*

OPPOSITE TOP LEFT: *Midnight blue bridesmaids' gowns are enhanced by the delightful bouquets in vibrant colors.*
Flowers: Hearts Bloom. Photo: Mark Papay
RIGHT: *A sensitive moment.*
PHOTO: *Durango Steele.*
BOTTOM LEFT: *Chivalrous groom kisses his bride's hand. Photo: Durango Steele.*
RIGHT: *Flower girl peeks through the crowd.*
PHOTO: *Baron Erik Spafford.*

FOLLOWING PAGE: *The attendant's attire complements the color scheme of the Allyson Brooke Newman and Jay Sachs' wedding.*
PHOTO: *John Reilly.*

ABOVE: *THIS RADIANT BRIDE WEARS A GOWN OF WHITE SILK AND SATIN BODICE WITH A TULLE SKIRT, ILLUSION SLEEVES AND A RHINESTONE-DOTTED COLLAR. BRIDESMAIDS WEAR DRAMATIC BLACK VELVET, IN A COMPLEMENTARY STYLE. FLOWER GIRLS IN FLUFFY WHITE TULLE SKIRTS AND VELVET TOPS CARRY NOSEGAYS OF LARGE WHITE ROSES. FLOWERS: DAVID BROWN FLOWERS. BELOW: NEWLYWEDS GRACE AND DOUG RABOLD LEAVE THE RITZ CARLTON, HOUSTON, TX, THROUGH A SHOWER OF BUBBLES AND PINK TISSUE HEARTS. WEDDING COORDINATED BY: THOMAS AND THOMAS. PHOTOS: ALVIN GEE*

THE BRIDESMAIDS' DRESSES

Until very recently, choices in bridesmaids' attire were limited. Fortunately, there is a small but growing revolution among the designers of bridesmaids' gowns. These designers are creating more sophisticated dresses designed to flatter the average woman's figure. Today, the choice of color and fabrics is expansive and, in fact, many brides now select black or white bridesmaids' dresses. When you look over your options, try to envision how your bridesmaids will look in the

photographs, and choose a style and color you think will complement everyone.

If you can't find bridesmaids' dresses you like in bridal salons, try fine department stores or specialty shops. Perhaps you'll encounter a line of dresses constructed of the same fabric but designed in several different styles. Or, if your wedding is not too formal, you may simply ask your bridesmaids to select a dress in a particular color and style, without insisting that the gowns be identical.

118

ATTIRE FOR THE MEN

Men's wedding attire is dictated by the formality of the wedding and by the style and color of the bride's gown. The groom, groomsmen, and bride's father should be dressed in similar suits, although the groom may want to add a few touches that make him stand out from the others—perhaps a colorful waistcoat or tie. He may also wear a boutonniere that's a different color from those worn by the ushers.

Formal weddings give men a rare opportunity to dress like the lord of the manor they may secretly aspire to be. The traditional evening outfit includes a full-dress tailcoat with matching trousers, white waistcoat, white bow tie, and wing-collared shirt. A black top hat and white gloves can be worn by the dedicated clotheshorse. A daytime formal wedding might call for a cutaway coat, gray striped trousers, gray waistcoat, wing-collared shirt, and ascot or striped tie. A top hat, spats, and gray gloves finish off the ensemble for those inclined to finery.

Not every would-be manor lord has a cutaway coat and waistcoat hanging in the closet, but not to worry. In most weddings the groom, best man, and even fathers rent their formal wear. There are a wide selection of tuxedos and suits available for rental, so shop around for the store that offers the best quality

Heidi Mauracher

at a reasonable price. If possible, rent everything from the same shop, and if you can't, at least get the same type of suit for the groom and attendants. Consider having the groom's father dress in the same attire as the attendants, since it will make for a more consistent overall look in the wedding photos. The bride's father always dresses in the prescribed wedding suit.

At a less formal wedding, the male attendants can wear suits as opposed to tuxedos, but they must be similar to one another in style and color. For evening or winter weddings, navy, black, or dark gray is generally worn. A white or ivory suit can be worn for summer afternoons. If the groom's suit is white or ivory, it should match the bride's dress; if she wears ivory, he should not wear stark white.

Informal weddings and theme weddings free the groom to be as fanciful as he likes. I've seen men stride down the aisle in Edwardian suits, Scottish kilts, and jeans and cowboy boots. Mountain-bike designer, Charlie Cunningham and his bride, bike racer Jacquie Phelan, were wed outdoors in customized cycle gear: black bicycle shorts and tuxedo shirt for him, white bicycle shorts and a frilly lace shirt for her. Passion and a sense of fun are what make your wedding unique.

very cute, are too young to understand what's going on. Their antics can be amusing, but they may simply distract from the moment.

It's not necessary to have either a ring bearer or a train bearer, but if you know one or two little boys about four or five years old, you may want to let them take part. The ring bearer or train bearer may also be a little girl, dressed the same way as the flower girls. Their duties are minimal, but they look adorable.

LEFT: *Flower girl, Lauren, lovingly kisses her brother, Nicholas.*
PHOTO: *Brian Kramer*
BELOW: *Sometimes weddings test everyone's patience.*
PHOTO: *Denis Reggie*

OPPOSITE: *A kiss and a hug for good luck.* PHOTO: *Brian Kramer*

FLOWER GIRLS AND RING BEARERS

The tradition of flower girls goes back many centuries, and it's easy to see why—they're irresistible. In ancient days, young children sprinkled herbs and grains before the bride as she walked, to encourage the gods to bless her with fertility. Today, girls carrying baskets of flowers precede the bride down the aisle, scattering rose petals as they go.

Most little girls adore being selected for this very special duty. If your family is large, please consider the feelings of all the little girls who may wish to be among the chosen few. Brides typically select one or two girls between the ages of four and eight years old. If you have two, it's visually pleasing to choose girls who are about the same size. Tiny tots, although

Tokens of Thanks

Giving small presents to those in the wedding party is a time-honored tradition. In the past, white kid-leather gloves were presented to the bridesmaids. Today, you might surprise your attendants with engraved silver perfume bottles or keepsake boxes made of plush brocade. A set of top-quality makeup brushes is always appreciated, as are more practical gifts such as leather-bound appointment books or fine writing instruments. Personalized gifts, such as hand-embroidered sachets are a memorable way to show your bridesmaids that you value their friendship and support.

For the groomsmen, silver business-card holders, pen-and-pencil sets, and even tickets to sporting events are welcome surprises.

OPPOSITE: *Young attendants bring innocence to this charming bridal party. Photo: Claudia Kunin. Satin ribbon winds gracefully around the handle of this lovely basket of roses and petals. Photo: G. Gregory Geiger. A little time for reflection. Photo: Durango Steele. Simple organza transforms this chair. Festive gold ribbon secures sprigs of Eucalyptus. Styled by Hearts Bloom.*

THIS PAGE

ABOVE LEFT: *Delightful ring bearers and flower girls catch a ride on a golf cart. Photo: Durango Steele.*

ABOVE RIGHT: *Porch swing provides a lovely settee for this flower girl. Photo: Madearis Studio*

RIGHT: *Last-minute instructions for the flower girls. Photo: Kevin Hyde*

YOUR WEDDING GOWN

Your big moment will soon be here. This is the one day in your life when you want to look as beautiful as you possibly can with just the right hairstyle, the perfect makeup, and a dazzling, supremely flattering gown. Perhaps you know exactly what you want, and your only challenge is to find a gown that matches your fantasy. Or, you might have an entirely open mind about the dress, in which case you'll need to narrow your vision or be prepared to wander for months in the vast, white-satin realms of bridal salons.

SELECTING THE PERFECT GOWN

Believe it or not, white wedding gowns are a relatively recent tradition. Prior to the mid-1800s, a bride in America or Europe might just as likely have worn mauve, blue, soft gray, russet, or plum. Still today, in Asia, red signifies good tidings and is the traditional color for bridal dresses. Spanish brides of the Roman Catholic faith donned elaborate gowns of black lace. Blues, purples, and pastels were commonly worn by brides in both the Old World and the New World, until the day in 1840 when Queen Victoria wed Prince Albert. Her all-white ensemble, crowned by a wreath of diamonded-laced orange blossoms, set the new standard for wedding attire from that day.

Although brides have dressed in white for more than a hundred years, the silhouette of the gown has changed from decade to decade. At the dawn of the twentieth century, Edwardian fashion held sway, with leg-of-mutton sleeves and cinched-in waists. During the 1920s, the flapper look was reflected in long-waisted wedding frocks, embroidered with bugle beads. By the 1940s, however, the extravagant, full-skirted wedding gown was back in vogue. Inspired by Hollywood, the Cinderella gown became ingrained in the public's mind as the ultimate in romantic style.

Today, many brides still opt for a full skirt and long train, but this is by no means your only choice. You may wear any type of gown that suits your

ABOVE: *Peter Fox bridal shoes. Photo: Sunday Hendrickson.* LEFT: *Authentic sixpence slips into the bride's shoe to bring good luck. Beverly Clark Collection.* BELOW: *Beautifully detailed lace sleeve and glove. Photo: Baron Erik Spafford*

Denis Reggie

fancy and figure, as long as it blends well with the style of your wedding. A summer garden wedding calls for a very different type of dress than a formal church ceremony. An elaborate Victorian gown will look out-of-place in a contemporary synagogue. In all likelihood, however, your taste in setting will naturally carry through to your taste in wedding gowns.

There are a few other things to consider when choosing a gown. The season will, in part, determine your decision of fabric and style, as will the formality of the wedding. Your religion may have guidelines, too. Some places of worship may frown on bare shoulders or revealing gowns, so check with your clergy before buying your dress. Above all, choose a dress that flatters you.

The choices are endless, so it's a good idea to bring your mother or a friend along on your shopping excursions. Make sure your companion is someone whose taste you respect and whom you trust to give an honest opinion. Don't complicate the process by bringing a different person each time.

Before you make your first visit to a bridal salon, do some homework. Start by looking through the latest issues of bridal magazines, clipping the pictures of the dresses you like best. Note the name of the manufacturer on each picture, for easy reference later. Don't forget the back of the gown—all eyes will be focused on it as you stand at the altar and walk down the aisle. I advise brides to bring along any special accessories that will be part of the final ensemble—necklace, earrings, perhaps a pair of heirloom gloves.

Begin the search for your gown at least four to six months before the wedding. It may take you weeks to make a decision. You should allow the salon twelve to sixteen weeks to deliver the dress, after which it will need to be fitted. Bridal salons stock dozens, sometimes hundreds, of sample gowns, and finding the right one can be overwhelming. It's easiest if you enlist the aid of a sales consultant. She can narrow the selection for you by showing you appropriate dresses, once you've discussed your budget, the date and type of your wedding, and the style of dress you prefer.

PHOTO: CHRISTIANA CEPPAS. GOWN BY NANCY TAYLOR

OPPOSITE: *English pavilion. Photo: Heidi Mauracher.* LEFT TOP: *Elizabethan lace gown. Photo: Brian Kramer.* CENTER AND BOTTOM: *Photos: Fred Marcus Photography.* ABOVE: *Photo: Durango Steele*

THE VEIL OR HEADPIECE

A veil of tulle, falling softly over the bride's face and flowing past her shoulders, presents an unforgettably lovely picture. Long a symbol of modesty, the veil also connotes purity. Silhouetted against a sunlit chapel doorway, a veiled bride seems somehow to represent all women who have ever poised at the threshold of married life.

Veils may be purchased at bridal salons, or you may have one designed especially for your gown. Heirloom veils often feature exquisite lace and beading. If there are none in your family, a search of the antique clothing stores in your area might turn up something breathtaking.

If a veil doesn't suit your personality or the style of your wedding, there are a host of enchanting alternatives. Flowered wreaths, stylish hats adorned with silk blossoms, sumptuous bows, satin headbands embroidered with pearls and rhinestones; there are no limits to the creations that can enhance your wedding ensemble. Fresh flowers woven into the hair with silk ribbons are particularly popular in the summer months. Try on several styles before you decide on your headpiece, and consult your hairdresser as well. Bring along a close friend or your mother to help you make the final decision. Be certain that in addition to feeling comfortable in the headpiece, you'll be able to fasten it securely to your head. You don't want to spend the ceremony worrying that it will slip!

OPPOSITE: *Photo: Claudia Kunin*

THIS PAGE: *Photos: Durango Steele*

131

133

WEDDING ACCESSORIES

The perfect dress needs the perfect accessories—and they're a lot of fun to shop for.

Shoes and stockings. Your shoes should be not only sexy but sensible; you'll be on your feet for hours, dancing and mingling with your guests. A wise choice is a silk or satin pump that can be dyed to match your gown. You can dress the pumps up by covering them with matching lace or by attaching a jeweled clip to each shoe. (Clips are available in many fine shoe or department stores).

Depending on the couple's height relationship, some brides wear ballet slippers. These can be purchased at bridal salons or dance stores. The humble ballet slipper can rise to the occasion of a wedding if you have it covered in lace, studded with baby pearls, or appliquéd with satin roses.

Jewelry. It's best to keep your jewelry simple: you don't want it to compete with your dress. If the neckline of your gown is open, a single pendant or strand of pearls may complement the dress perfectly. Diamond or pearl earrings are elegant choices. If you don't own anything appropriate, you might ask a friend to loan you a pair. Something must be borrowed, after all!

ABOVE: *Embroidered satin wedding slippers.*
PHOTO: *Durango Steele*
CENTER: *Fashionably stylish, elaborately beaded bridal handbags. Beverly Clark Collection*

OPPOSITE: *Rich Venise lace ringbearer pillow with embroidered scalloped edge organza ruffle, heart-shaped box, pearled lace guest book, and champagne flute. Beverly Clark Collection.*
BELOW: *Tatted lace garter with ribbon accent. Photo: Madearis Studio*

Gloves. Long gloves may be worn with a sleeveless formal gown or if the gown's sleeves are short. Short gloves are generally worn with longer sleeved gowns. Make sure you've removed the glove on your left hand in time for the ring to be placed on your finger.

Garters. Delicate lace garters are often sold in shades of blue to comply with the "something blue" directive that nearly every bride follows religiously. One garter may be tossed to the single men at the reception, so buy two—you'll treasure this keepsake always.

Something Blue. The color blue has long been a symbol of purity, fidelity, hope, and love. In the early days of Judaism, brides wove blue ribbons into their hair. Perhaps this is where the "something blue" tradition began. If you don't wear a blue garter, there are other ways to incorporate the color into your ensemble. Use a hankie trimmed in blue, or you might wear a piece of jewelry with a sapphire stone. In England, it's the custom to tie streamers of blue-and-white knotted ribbon to corsages worn by the wedding party. You could tie some to your own bouquet, or simply include a few blue blossoms in the mix.

$\mathcal{F}$LOWERS

T HE USE OF FLOWERS to adorn the bride and brighten the wedding celebration is as old as marriage itself. In fact, nearly every type of blossom bears a symbolism that goes back for centuries. Flowering quince was favored by the ancient Greeks, who believed it would nurture the love between a bride and groom, while the Romans braided wreaths of marigolds and roses to guarantee love and longevity. Though flowers may speak differently to different cultures, people everywhere regard them with reverence.

Women take flowers personally. Many will confess that they've always been drawn to a certain blossom that they feel reflects their personality. Some love roses, while others are entranced by the confetti-like hues of summer poppies. Flowers may be lush or delicate, pale or dazzling.

Many of the romantic associations we have with flowers can be traced to the Victorian era. England's Queen Victoria reigned from 1837 to 1901, and during that period courtship became an intensely convoluted process. Men and women were not allowed to openly admit their feelings for each other, so they developed secret codes to express themselves. The flutter of a fan could signal the smallest nuance of desire, and calling cards carried multilayered messages. Flowers provided an even more eloquent means of communication. A lady could indicate ardor with red roses and jealousy with yellow, and with a variegated pink bloom she could refuse a suitor altogether. A gentleman could use flowers to sing a woman's praises without uttering a word: lilies praised her purity, white roses her innocence. Lilacs represented a first romance. Flowers were used to declare love and to spurn it, to tease and to implore. The traces of this intricate language are still evident in the meanings we attach to different blossoms today.

SELECTING A FLORIST

Because flowers are such an important element of the wedding, I always advise brides to start interviewing florists three or four months before the wedding date. If you live in a small town, the most gifted florists are usually booked early. As with every service, this is particularly true for weddings that will take place in the summer months.

Ask for recommendations of florists from your friends or from your caterer or any other wedding professional whose opinion you trust. It's best to work with someone who specializes in weddings and has a creative flair you respond to. Look through the florist's portfolio to experience the styles he or

PREVIOUS PAGE: *Presentation style bouquet of heather, lilacs, lisianthus, Kyria roses and white freesia. Photo: Baron Erik Spafford.* ABOVE: *tulips, freesia, astilbe, iris, roses, Asiatic lilies and Queen Ann's Lace create this lovely English garden bouquet. Photo: G. Gregory Geiger.* OPPOSITE: *Clutch bouquet with viburnum, stocks, roses, and sweet peas. Photo: G. Gregory Geiger. Flowers by The Flower Basket.*

she creates and discuss your desires early to be sure the florist can work within your budget.

Before the initial interview, collect photos, books, and magazine pictures that will help you give the florist a feel for the colors and styles you want. If possible, also bring swatches of the fabrics you're planning to use. A typical interview lasts about two hours. The florist will ask you how you envision the wedding and will discuss such practical items as the number of bouquets and centerpieces you'll need.

While you're chatting, make sure the florist knows what areas of the event are most important to you. For example, do you envision making a dramatic entrance? If so, the florist should pay attention to the aisle decorations or to the staircase down which you'll descend. If you're more

interested in creating an elaborate reception, the florist should concentrate on that. Unless your budget is unlimited, you'll have to set these types of priorities.

At the first meeting, most of the concepts should be worked out and a tentative budget set. You'll want to get everything in writing, down to the names and colors of every flower. At a second meeting, scheduled closer to the wedding date, you'll finalize such details as the colors in the bridesmaid's bouquets, which are dependent on the shade of their dresses.

Joni Papay, owner of Hearts Bloom in Santa Barbara, California, has designed wedding flowers for twenty years. During her initial interview with a couple, Joni tries to discover something unique about them that will inspire her and make their celebration especially meaningful. In one wedding, the key element was a sheer chiffon tablecloth appliquéd with roses. It had been a gift from the bride's beloved grandmother, who had recently passed away. Hearts Bloom built a four-columned *chuppah* for the ceremony and tied a corner of the tablecloth to the tip of each column to create the ceremonial canopy. "Everyone got quite emotional

OPPOSITE FAR LEFT: *Uncomplicated, petite nosegay of stephanotis, freesia and tea roses, finished with three companion ribbons. Stems have been wrapped with ribbon, extending the expression. Photo: Sidney Cooper*
LEFT: *Loosely gathered white roses with tulle and seed pearls. Flowers: Hearts Bloom. Photo: Durango Steele*

THIS PAGE LEFT: *Herb garden favorites contribute to a very elegant bouquet that includes thyme, roses and curly willow tied with golden ribbon. Flowers: Hearts Bloom. Photo: Mark Papay. BELOW: Cascade of roses, orchids, eucalyptus and wax flower. An addition of yarrow adds fragrance and softens the bouquet. Photo: Joann Pecoraro*

when they saw it," says Joni. "It was like Grandma was looking down on them." The flowers that entwined the columns and filled the centerpieces were, of course, roses.

"The element of surprise is what makes flowers memorable," says Joni. She's designed a floral purse, floral shoes, and flower-entwined music stands. "People are used to seeing flowers at the altar or in centerpieces. But a floral purse is something they'll really notice and remember. That's what the brides I work with are looking for, above all else: something different."

WHICH FLOWERS ARE RIGHT FOR YOU?

Your wedding gown is a good starting point for selecting your bouquet flowers. The bouquet should carry out the style of the gown and, most importantly, should not outdazzle you. The size of the bouquet depends on two things: the size of the bride and the style of gown. An extremely elaborate bridal gown demands a somewhat extravagant bouquet, while a simpler dress would be better served by a more delicate, understated arrangement. Likewise, petite brides are complemented by smaller bouquets, while larger ladies can carry a more generous and striking design.

Now is the time to indulge yourself in the flowers you adore, those that have a special, personal meaning for you or whose scent has always lifted your spirits. Your bouquet can easily complement the rest of your wedding flowers without containing exactly the same blossoms. You might therefore like to select exotic, imported flowers that would be too costly to use on a larger scale.

If you want to keep your bouquet for sentimental reasons, make sure you order a "tossing bouquet." This can be an exact duplicate of the real thing or a smaller, less expensive version. Adding long ribbon streamers to the tossing bouquet will make the flower toss that much more visually exciting. As I mentioned in an earlier chapter, a bride will often ask her florist to create a tossing bouquet that looks like the bridal bouquet her mother carried when she was wed.

The practical bride will bear in mind that flowers in season at the time of her wedding will be more affordable and easier to find than flowers that are not. Of course, with hothouse cultivation and shipping by air, you can get almost anything in any month—for a price. But before you write that check, ask your florist about substitutions. It just may be that there are alternate choices that will look even more breathtaking than the flowers you wanted originally.

OPPOSITE AND THIS PAGE: *PHOTOS: DURANGO STEELE*

FAVORITE WEDDING FLOWERS

We usually associate roses with weddings. Their intoxicating fragrance, stunning range of hues, and romantic history make them the ideal wedding bloom. But another flower has graced bride and her event for even longer: the orange blossom. These small, white blooms smell divine, although the scent usually fades during shipping. The orange tree produces both fruit and flowers at the same time and

stays green all year long, suggesting a union that is perennially fruitful and vibrant. This metaphor has not been lost on brides, who for centuries have included orange blossoms in their wedding wreaths and bouquets. On the day she wed Prince Albert, Queen Victoria herself glowed beneath a crown of orange blossoms woven with diamonds.

All of the most popular flowers are associated with some noble or desirable quality. The list below includes some favorite wedding flowers and their special meanings.

Apple blossom — good fortune
Baby's breath — pure heart
Blue violet — faithfulness
Bluebell — constancy
Carnation — distinction
Chrysanthemum — friendship
Daffodil — joy
Daisy — loyalty
Forget-me-not — true love
Forsythia — anticipation
Gardenia — joy
Gladiolus — generosity
Iris — wisdom
Ivy — fidelity
Lily — purity and innocence
Lily of the valley — happiness
Magnolia — nobility
Orange blossom — purity and fertility
Orchid — beauty
Peony — happiness
Rose — deep love
Stephanotis — happiness in marriage
Sweetpeas — delicate pleasures
White daisy — innocence
Zinnia — goodness

OPPOSITE AND THIS PAGE: *FLOWERS: FLEURS.* PHOTO: *G. GREGORY GEIGER*

THE BRIDAL BOUQUET

Choosing the flowers for your bouquet is perhaps the most pleasant of all pre-wedding tasks. It's quite likely that your ideal bouquet can easily be created, and even improved upon, with the help of a talented florist. Clipping photographs from magazines or bringing along a book with pictures of bouquets is an excellent way to make sure the florist understands what you want.

As you browse through these sources, you might be struck by the variety of bouquets they display.

Today's abundant selection reflects every style of wedding bouquet seen over the past five centuries, as well as some delightfully modern versions.

Bridal bouquets began in medieval times as nosegays—small, sweet-smelling clusters carried by medieval brides. The bouquets expanded in size over the centuries, largely to keep pace with ever more extravagant wedding gowns. The nosegay grew to be a larger, full, round bouquet held by a silver horn, called a tussie-mussie. This larger mound of flowers, usually white, was framed by a circle of ferns. Finally, this type of bouquet blossomed into the cascade, a

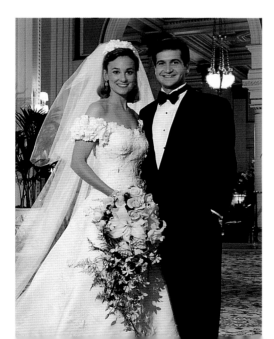

stupendous display of dozens of white blooms that draped down almost to the bride's hemline.

The 1930s ushered in a new wave of bouquet designs. The fashion was Art Deco, and long, slender flowers, or perhaps a single calla lily, complemented the sleek lines of the wedding gowns. Bridal bouquets since that time have mirrored the fortunes and trends of the day. Perhaps the most influential period of recent years was the 1970s, with its focus on a natural look. Wildflowers and loosely gathered bouquets fit right in with the more relaxed weddings of that time. This freedom of expression can still be seen twenty years later. Rules about wedding bouquets have all but vanished, leaving brides free to design any sort of bouquet they like. Flowers are no longer limited to white or cream, although pale blossoms are often chosen because they fit the spirit of the occasion and don't draw attention from the bride.

A recent trend is to simply hand-tie a mass of like-colored roses with ribbon, so that they look graceful yet unpretentious. The simple, just-picked look has been extremely popular for the past several years, and its

CASCADING CENTERPIECE OF WHITE ROSES, DENDROBIUM ORCHIDS, BABY'S BREATH AND IVY SURROUND TAPER CANDLES WITH GOLD CORDING AND TASSEL ACCENTS. PHOTO: CLAY BLACKMORE

appeal is understandable: an armful of flowers gathered in a loose bouquet indeed makes a charming sight. Some brides, though, yearn for a more elaborate look. Also in vogue are striking cascades of Dendrobium orchids mixed with roses, peonies, gardenias, and lilies of the valley.

Some brides find it hard to resist adding a bit of color to their bouquets, most often blue or lavender. Lilacs and hydrangea are popular choices here. Fall weddings seem to inspire even bolder palettes: burgundy roses arranged with pale, peach-colored blooms make for a stunning and very romantic bouquet. Red roses and poinsettias are always popular for holiday weddings

A small back-to-the-herbs movement is taking place today, marking a return to the medieval bouquets mentioned earlier. An herb bouquet, which also contains flowers, might include a combination of sage, lemon balm, lavender, rosemary, orchids, and twigs. It smells heavenly and will make a wonderful keepsake. Although herbs will never take the place of flowers, for many brides these bouquets offer a sweet alternative to the standard rose-and-lily arrangements.

ABOVE LEFT: *Fragrant gardenia cascade. Photo: T.G. McCary*

ABOVE: *Bridal cascade of tea roses, Cattleya orchids, stephanotis and freesia.*
Photo: G. Gregory Geiger.

LEFT: *Hand-tied bouquet of tuber rose, bridal white, blush pink and Vivaldi roses,*
accented with a gorgeous silk organza ribbon. Flowers:: Hearts Bloom. Photo: Mark Papay

FLOWERS FOR BRIDESMAIDS AND FLOWER GIRLS

The blossoms carried by bridesmaids and flower girls are usually more vibrant in color than those in the bridal bouquet. These bouquets should be harmonious with the rest of the floral wedding displays, such as centerpieces and altar arrangements, as well as with the bridesmaids' gowns.

Often, some of the same flowers are used in both the bride's and the attendants' bouquets, although the tones may be different. The bride might carry pale blush and

Flower girls carry flowers, of course—usually baskets of rose petals that the girls scatter as they walk down the aisle. If there is more than one flower girl, or if your house of worship doesn't allow petals, the flower girls may carry small nosegays.

PRESERVING YOUR BOUQUET

Bridal bouquets are difficult to part with—hence the popularity of tossing bouquets. Luckily, there are several ways you can preserve your wedding bouquet.

Your florist can preserve the bouquet in its entirety

ivory roses, while the bridesmaids' roses are a deep peach color. Until recently, bridesmaids' bouquets have been much less elaborate than the one carried by the bride. Today, bridesmaids' bouquets are often just as beautiful as the bride's, but in stronger colors and slightly smaller.

Flower girls usually wear wreaths made of the same blossoms used elsewhere in the wedding. The girls' delicate features may be enhanced by using buds or miniature species rather than full-sized flowers, especially if the featured wedding blossoms are large. Baby's breath and ferns add a soft look to the wreaths, while ribbons provide a romantic touch.

through a process in which the moisture is removed and the flowers are sprayed with a protective solution. The preserved bouquet can be displayed in a shadow box or glass case, or it can be stored for posterity. You can preserve the bouquet yourself by placing it in a box and completely covering it with borax or silica gel. This process usually takes about a week.

Another method of preservation is to press the flowers individually. This method, which takes about six weeks, is commonly done if the bouquet is to be framed. You can ask your florist for tips on this technique or buy a book on the subject. Pressing basically involves

OPPOSITE: *Bridal bouquet is highlighted by all white, fully-opened garden roses, while the bridesmaids carry white and pink spray roses with white lisianthius and pittosporum greenery. Photo: Heidi Mauraucher.*

Lovely floral head wreath of baby spray roses and ivy. Floral wreath: Scott Hogue.

ABOVE LEFT: *The presentation bouquet for this Matron of Honor uses lighter shades of pinks and red to complement her outfit. Included are tulips, Vivaldi roses, bouvardia and la Reve lilies tied with French ribbon.* ABOVE RIGHT: *Very colorful bridal bouquet of white Casablanca lilies, deep pink and orange tulips, tuberoses and alstroemeria. Flowers: Hearts Bloom. Photos: Mark Papay*

ABOVE: *Bridal bouquet filled with peonies and tied with silk organza ribbon (Left). Bridesmaid's bouquet of roses and seeded eucalyptus with contrasting ribbon (Right). Flowers: Hearts Bloom*

ABOVE RIGHT: *Round bouquet of Osiana roses.*

RIGHT: *A bouquet that is both fragrant and colorful with roses, alstroemeria, hand tied with damask ribbon. Flowers: Hearts Bloom Photos: Michael Garland*

FAR RIGHT: *Heart shaped bridal bouquet with white and Dendrobium orchids, tuberoses and roses. Flowers: Hearts Bloom Photo: Mark Papay*

JONI PAPAY OF HEARTS BLOOM CREATED THIS STUNNING CHAIR GARLAND FOR
THE BRIDE'S AND GROOM'S CHAIRS, MADE FROM MORE THAN 200 ROSES, USING FOUR TYPES:
BRIDAL WHITE, ISABELLA SPRAY, PORCELANA, AND OSIANA. THE GARLAND WAS THEN TIED
TO THE CHAIR WITH GOLD MESH RIBBON. PHOTO: MICHAEL GARLAND

separating the bouquet, then placing the blossoms beneath heavy objects such as books, or putting them in a flower press. Getting a few tips from the experts first will likely give you a more beautifully pressed bouquet.

HEADPIECES AND FLORAL WREATHS

A flowered headpiece or wreath can be a lovely addition to your wedding ensemble. A classic wreath of lilies of the valley and baby spray roses enhances an impression of youth and liveliness, while more unusual wreaths can complement many types of gowns.

Flowers near your face can make your skin seem rosier or your eyes brighter. For a bride with curly blond hair and light blue eyes, Joni Papay designed a wreath of baby blue delphiniums with a pouf of tulle in the back for a veil. If a wreath is not your style, the Bud Clip™ offers an ideal alternative. The hair clip features 1, 2 or 3 tiny water vials, hidden by intricate sculpturing, that keep the flowers fresh during the hours of your celebration. The Bud Clip™ can be configured to hold your veil during the ceremony, and then later may replace your headpiece during the reception.

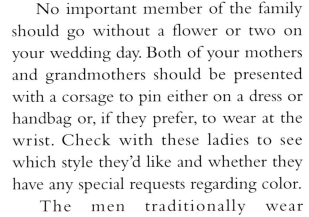

THIS BUD PIN IS A SPECIALLY DESIGNED HOLDER FOR A FRESH FLOWER BOUTONNIERE. PHOTO: CLAUDIA KUNIN

CHAMPAGNE ROSE NOSEGAY BY LAURELS CUSTOM FLORIST WRAPPED IN ALTERNATING RIBBON KNOTS. PHOTO: AMEDEO. WHITE ROSES AND TULLE DECORATE THIS HAT. FLOWERS: HEARTS BLOOM. PHOTO: MARK PAPAY.

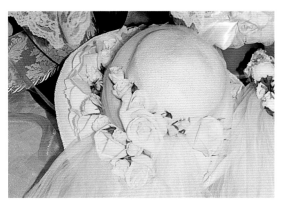

BLOOMS FOR THE FAMILIES AND THE GROOM

No important member of the family should go without a flower or two on your wedding day. Both of your mothers and grandmothers should be presented with a corsage to pin either on a dress or handbag or, if they prefer, to wear at the wrist. Check with these ladies to see which style they'd like and whether they have any special requests regarding color.

The men traditionally wear boutonnieres, generally a single blossom such as a rosebud or perhaps a shaft of lilies of the valley. All of the groomsmen's boutonnieres are alike, but the groom wears something a little more special.

FLOWERS FOR THE CEREMONY

Indoors or outdoors, intimate country chapel or breathtaking cathedral...the setting of your ceremony has everything to do with which flowers you choose. After that, your budget will determine how far you can go to beautify the site with flowers.

For indoor ceremonies that take place in a house of worship, floral displays are usually set up at the ends of the pews, the altar,

TOP ROW: *Delightful floral brooches can replace mothers' corsages and make wonderful keepsakes. Flowers: Hearts Bloom. Photo: Mark Papay.* LEFT: *Floral brooch of hydrangea, eucalyptus and pearls.* CENTER: *Roses, pearls and shells make a pretty brooch combination.* RIGHT: *Gold tassel, hydrangea and seed eucalyptus brooch.* ABOVE: *Tea Rose flower girl basket with blush rose petals. Basket from Beverly Clark Collection. Photo: Henry Hamamoto*

RIGHT: *Roses and baby's breath tied with ribbons enhance the innocence of these little sweethearts.*

Floral wreaths: Atlas Floral Decorators.

Photo: Fred Marcus Photography

and the *chuppah* or arch. Traditionally associated with Jewish weddings, *chuppahs* are becoming popular in all denominations. They provide a picturesque frame for the couple as they stand at the altar, and in a large space they convey shelter and warmth.

You'll need to take into account the size and style of your setting when deciding what sorts of flowers will work best. At the breathtaking Wayfarer's Chapel in Palos Verdes, California, the wall behind the altar is an enormous expanse of glass overlooking a wooded scene. In the face of such an extraordinary natural display, understated greenery and a few well-chosen blooms will most likely enhance the setting. Conversely, a space that is dark or has relatively little decoration will benefit from grand displays of exquisite flowers and candles that add a romantic glow.

Pew arrangements range from the extravagant to the small but tasteful. Lavish ribboned wreaths, exquisite topiaries, and lush garlands create a sense of opulence and occasion. However, the budget-minded can decorate to great effect for far fewer dollars by embellishing only every third or fourth pew, and by being creative. For example, the arrangements can be made less expensive but no less beautiful by using more ribbons and greenery and fewer flowers. Here's a chance as well to use eucalyptus or rosemary, whose fragrance will add to the ambiance of the room. Or, if the season permits, snip branches from a flowering

cherry or apple tree and use them as pew decorations. Christmas weddings can make use of holly or pine boughs, which are also wonderfully aromatic.

For the altar, think large. Small, delicate arrangements will get lost, and anything too low will be hidden from the audience's view. Here, too, flowering branches may be used by the budget-conscious bride. Bold, graphic displays in brilliant hues or living trees such as the ficus are large enough to make a visual impression on those seated in the back rows.

Chuppahs are often created using a frame upon which fabric, greenery, and flowers are arranged. Larger blossoms work better here, too, as delicate blossoms might fade to a blur past the first few pews.

Your house of worship may have specific rules for placement of flowers. Check before planning your floral decorations.

Outdoor weddings require a much different approach to flowers. Simply put, there's no point in competing with nature. An arch or a canopy adds a nice touch to an outdoor wedding, as it delineates the ceremony area and provides a focal point. Again, it must be bold enough to make a visual statement in the great outdoors.

ABOVE: *Aisle treatment of garden roses and dendrobium orchids by Scott Hogue.*
OPPOSITE: *Elaborate chuppah of white moiré fabric and handmade gold tassels designed by Hearts Bloom. Photos: Durango Steele.*

OPPOSITE: *ARCH OF HUCKLEBERRY GREENERY BUILDS THE FRAME TO HOLD COLORFUL FLOWERS.*
PHOTO: PETER DIGGS. BELOW: BOXES OF ROSE PETALS WERE USED TO CREATE A BEAUTIFULLY FRAGRANT AISLE RUNNER. FLOWERS: FLORAMOR STUDIOS

ABOVE: *TOPIARIES AND TULLE GLORIFY THIS AISLE, WITH A MATCHING SPRAY OVER THE ARCH*
BELOW: *SHOWERS OF ROSE PETALS, TOSSED BY GUESTS.*
PHOTOS: DURANGO STEELE.
LEFT: *DECORATED ENGLISH CHIPPENDALE ARCH.*
FLOWERS: HEARTS BLOOM. PHOTO: MARK PAPAY

159

CLAUDIA KUNIN

FLOWERS FOR THE RECEPTION

Nowhere are flowers more important than at the reception. They set the mood and express the essence of your wedding, be it romantic or playful, elegant or magical. Your guests will be gazing around your reception for hours, and you want to provide them with a wonderful visual feast.

Centerpieces are the focal point of the tables at the reception. They must be either low enough for guests to see over or high enough to see under. Consider the size of the room when deciding on your centerpieces. If you feel somewhat dwarfed by the ceiling as you stand in the reception hall, you may want to use high centerpieces that will fit the scale of the room and create a lower visual "ceiling."

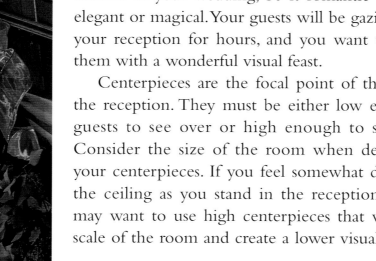

G. GREGORY GEIGER

G. GREGORY GEIGER

FLOWERS: FLORAMOR STUDIOS. PHOTO: ELIOT HOLTZMAN

A small room calls for low centerpieces that add to the mood of intimacy.

Centerpieces can include more than just flowers. Teapots of silver or hand-painted porcelain, stone urns, and ornate candelabras are just a few of the props that can add excitement or whimsy to the table. One penny-wise bride used miniature rose topiaries in gaily painted boxes as centerpieces. Later, she planted those same roses on the walkway to her front door. It's hard to imagine a happier reminder of a glorious wedding day.

Flowers can enhance every element of the reception. Florists often work closely with caterers to design clever and attractive displays of food and flowers for buffet tables. On the cake table, flowers can adorn not just the table but the cake itself. Many wedding cakes feature real flowers as opposed to sugar versions, and often boast a mixture of the two. Even humble chairs can be given a festive look with satin bows or lengths of tulle secured with greenery and a few fresh blossoms.

OPPOSITE AND TOP: FLOWERS: SCOTT HOGUE. PHOTOS: CLINT WEISMAN

CLAY BLACKMORE

G. GREGORY GEIGER. FLOWERS: FLORAL FEATS

ABOVE AND OPPOSITE: PHOTOS: CLAY BLACKMORE. FLOWERS: BARBARA TAYLOR FLORAL DESIGNS

OPPOSITE: G. GREGORY GEIGER

THE CEREMONY

THE CEREMONY is the soul of a wedding. The words with which you and your groom pledge your love and loyalty, and the setting in which this sacred pledge is spoken, will live in your memory forever. Many elements make up the ceremony: the vows, the procession, the roles of parents and attendants, and the house of worship or secular site where it all unfolds. The most important of these is the spiritual aspect, the vows themselves.

Although civil ceremonies have become commonplace over the past decade, many couples still want a priest or rabbi to preside over their vows. If you and your fiancé are of the same faith, you'll need to agree on where to hold the ceremony and who you'd like to have officiate. In Chapter Two, "Unique Weddings," you got a glimpse of places you could choose for the ceremony. In all but the most orthodox faiths, a clergy will be happy to marry you outside a house of worship.

RELIGIOUS CEREMONIES

Most priests and rabbis ask that the couple spend some time in premarital counseling prior to their wedding. This holds true for both same-faith and different-faith couples, as well as for those marrying for a second time.

You should be aware that most churches and temples have rules regarding acceptable gowns,

headgear, the use of photographic equipment, musicians, flowers, candles, and so forth. These guidelines must be respected, so be sure to inquire about them before setting your heart on a site.

CATHOLIC CEREMONIES

As with most religions, the Catholic Church views marriage as a serious and lasting commitment. Because marriage is one of the seven sacraments, most parishes require premarital counseling to help the couple prepare for their life together.

The church discourages weddings from taking place on Sundays or holy days. It also requires that traditional vows be recited, although slight changes

PREVIOUS PAGE: *Exquisite flowers and draped ribbon runners appoint the aisle for this church wedding. Flowers: Floramor Studios. Photo: Eliot Holtzman.* INSET AND BELOW: *Gold-covered bible and Greek ceremonial headpieces and candles. Photo: James D. Macari*

ABOVE: *In this Catholic ceremony the bride, groom, maid of honor and best man are seated at the altar. Attendants are seated to the left and right. Multiple arrangements in varying heights create a beautiful and fragrant focal point. Photo: G. Gregory Geiger.*

BELOW: *Pearl-decorated unity and taper candles sit atop column candle holders. Beverly Clark Collection*

may be acceptable as long as the meaning remains the same. The most traditional Catholic ceremony takes place at noon—a Nuptial Mass. Low Mass takes place at ten o'clock. The simplest of Catholic ceremonies, celebrated in the church without a mass, may take place in the afternoon.

Two symbolic rituals are often incorporated into the Catholic ceremony. In one, the bride places her bouquet at the shrine or statue of the Virgin Mary while a prayer is said; in the other, both bride and groom light one large unity candle from two smaller ones to signify their new life together.

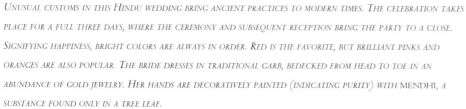

UNUSUAL CUSTOMS IN THIS HINDU WEDDING BRING ANCIENT PRACTICES TO MODERN TIMES. THE CELEBRATION TAKES PLACE FOR A FULL THREE DAYS, WHERE THE CEREMONY AND SUBSEQUENT RECEPTION BRING THE PARTY TO A CLOSE. SIGNIFYING HAPPINESS, BRIGHT COLORS ARE ALWAYS IN ORDER. RED IS THE FAVORITE, BUT BRILLIANT PINKS AND ORANGES ARE ALSO POPULAR. THE BRIDE DRESSES IN TRADITIONAL GARB, BEDECKED FROM HEAD TO TOE IN AN ABUNDANCE OF GOLD JEWELRY. HER HANDS ARE DECORATIVELY PAINTED (INDICATING PURITY) WITH MENDHI, A SUBSTANCE FOUND ONLY IN A TREE LEAF.

ABOVE: *Photo courtesy of Willows Whisp Country Club.* RIGHT: *Photos: Jennifer Drake*

EASTERN ORTHODOX CEREMONIES

The traditions of the Eastern rite churches, including Russian and Greek Orthodox, are similar in many ways to Catholic practices. The ceremony, long and full of symbolism, usually takes place in the afternoon or early evening, barring seasons of fasting or holy days.

The ceremony begins with a betrothal ritual in which rings are blessed, exchanged three times to signify the Holy Trinity, and then placed on the bride's and groom's right hand. At the close of the ritual, the bride and groom, each of whom wears a crown during the service, exchange their crowns three times. A Gospel is read, and the couple drinks from the same glass of wine three times. The ceremony concludes with the bride and groom, hands bound together, being led around a ceremonial table three times while the congregation sings "God Grant Them Many Years."

ABOVE: *A CATHOLIC DOUBLE-WEDDING CEREMONY FOR TWO SISTERS AND THEIR GROOMS TOOK PLACE AT HISTORIC OUR LADY OF MOUNT CARMEL CHAPEL IN MONTECITO, CA.*
PHOTO: *JAMES D. MACARI*

RIGHT: *EXTERIOR AND GARDENS OF OUR LADY OF MOUNT CARMEL CHAPEL.*
PHOTO: *DURANGO STEELE*

Protestant Ceremonies

While most Protestant churches have similar marriage ceremonies, each sect has its own practices and traditions. It is best to go over the regulations of the church with your clergy. Some are reluctant to perform marriages on Sundays or holy days, although technically it's allowed. Many churches will require the engaged couple to attend premarital counseling sessions.

In Protestant ceremonies the bride is escorted down the aisle and given away by her father. If he is not available, her mother, a brother, another relative, or a close friend may escort the bride, or she may choose to walk down the aisle alone. The father or escort is asked, "Who giveth this woman to be married to this man?" Traditionally, the father answers, "Her mother and I do." He then places his daughter's hand in the groom's hand, and takes his seat in the front left row. The marriage vows end with the words "until death do us part." Many go on to finish the ceremony with the Lord's Prayer.

ABOVE AND LEFT: *The evening wedding ceremony of Charlotte Ann Hall to Greg O'Neal took place at the Cathedral of St. Philip in Atlanta. She and her groom were joined at the altar by eighteen attendants, four flower girls and two ring bearers.*
PHOTO: *Kevin Hyde*

RIGHT: *Bride signing her wedding certificate.*
PHOTO: *Durango Steele*

ABOVE: *Extraordinary aisle runner in the hotel ballroom leads the eye to the fresh flower-trimmed* CHUPPAH (CANOPY) *during this Jewish ceremony.*

OPPOSITE: *After the ceremony, the same canopy spotlights the cake at the reception. Wedding design: Floramor Studios. Photos: Richard Miller*

Left photo: Brian Kramer

Opposite photo:

Bruce Forrester Photography.

Flowers: Floramor Studios

Jewish Ceremonies

The Jewish faith is composed of three branches: Orthodox, the most strict in observance of Jewish law; Conservative, in the middle; and Reform, the most liberal. The Jewish wedding may take place at any time except on the Sabbath (from sundown Friday to sundown on Saturday), during Passover, or on any other holy days.

In all three factions, the service is held in both Hebrew and English, though in a Reform ceremony, the Hebrew is minimal. Today, couples may opt to write their own vows in addition to the traditional promises. In an Orthodox ceremony, the bride circles the groom numerous times, corresponding to ancient custom. The ring is usually placed on the index finger of the bride's right hand during the ceremony, and later is switched to the left hand. Performed by a rabbi, beneath a *chuppah,* the ceremony ends with a reciting of the seven blessings.

Traditionally, the bride and groom share blessed wine from a wine goblet, which is then wrapped in a napkin and smashed beneath the groom's foot. This action, representing the destruction of the holy temple in Jerusalem in 70 B.C., also reminds the newlyweds of their obligation to Zion, and that even during the most joyous of occasions, they must remember that all of life is not happiness. Also, smashed glass cannot be reconstructed and so is a symbol that marriage is fragile and must be treated with respect. The smashing also harkens to days when cultures believed loud noises would ward off evil spirits.

BELOW: *Sword archway for the bride and groom. Photo: Weddings by Weintraub.* LOWER LEFT: *Giant Eucalyptus tree and sensational blooms catch the romance for this bride and groom. Photo: Durango Steele.* RIGHT: *Majestic waterfall at The Calabassas Inn offers a spectacular setting for this ceremony. Photo: Bennett Photography*

CIVIL CEREMONIES

A civil ceremony is performed by a judge or authorized official and may take place anywhere except a house of worship. Courthouse ceremonies are ideal for small, informal weddings. There's an appealing air of spontaneity at these affairs. After the ceremony, the wedding party usually celebrates at a small reception or a nearby restaurant.

Couples with religious differences often choose to be married by a judge. Civil ceremonies can be every bit as moving as those performed by a person of the cloth, especially since you are entirely

free to write your own vows. The rituals are basically identical to those of a religious ceremony following the same design. Choosing a civil ceremony can be a compelling alternative to negotiating the interfaith obstacle course, as long as you are both comfortable with it and your families are supportive.

PERSONALIZING YOUR CEREMONY

Standing before the altar, in front of your parents and all those who love you, is an extraordinary experience. Sometimes a bride and groom want to personalize these moments by adding to or altering the traditional ceremony wording. Kahlil Gibran's "On Marriage," from The Prophet, and certain poems by Walt Whitman have graced many a wedding ceremony. Solomon's "Song of Songs," from the Old Testament, is another favorite. Bookstores carry volumes of romantic poetry that can enrich your ceremony. Just reading through them can be an inspiring break from the busy pre-wedding pace.

Some couples elect to compose all or part of their own ceremony. By incorporating traditional elements with more personal sentiments, you can tailor your ceremony to exactly suit your passion and commitment. This can be a bit daunting, but you have nothing to lose by giving it a try. Some people want to speak during their ceremony, while others feel they'll be too emotional or are too shy to manage anything more than "I do." Most ministers, priests, and rabbis will gladly recite your lines with all the force and feeling you desire.

As you're composing your ceremony, keep in mind that the vows themselves should only take two or three minutes to recite to each other. Additional thoughts on your commitment to marriage may be expressed in the main body of the ceremony, through the use of special poems and prayers.

When you've finished writing the ceremony, give a typed copy to the officiant a few weeks before the date so he or she can become familiar with it. If you choose

Durango Steele

to recite part of it yourselves, be sure to keep a copy and go over it until you feel comfortable with the lines. Keep your speaking parts short. It's so easy to forget your lines in the excitement of the moment.

Some couples choose to face their guests rather than the altar as they exchange their vows. This is another way to make the ceremony unique and acknowledge your affection for your family and friends.

A printed program will add a touch of warmth to your ceremony, especially if your guests will be numerous. The program could include the names of your attendants, along with a few notes about who they are or how you met them; a special poem or prayer; the names of the musicians and the pieces they will perform; and your wedding vows.

Your Wedding Vows

In the rush to create a stunning event, the wedding's deeper meaning can sometimes be temporarily forgotten. Selecting or writing your vows will help center you again and give you and

your groom a chance to focus on those aspects that are truly important.

Strictly religious vows are still favored by many couples. These resonate with centuries of tradition, and given a few minor changes ("obey" is now routinely omitted, and "man and wife" have been replaced with "husband and wife"), they stand the test of time.

Ministers and rabbis often develop their own wedding services over the years, incorporating traditional phrases, favorite passages from the Bible, and other elements they have found to be especially moving or relevant. There will usually be a certain point during these ceremonies where it is appropriate for you to insert some words of your own, or a passage or poem that is meaningful to you.

Religious ceremonies break down into these basic components:

The welcome, or call to worship

A reading or prayer

The wedding meditation, consisting of the clergy's comments on the marriage

Declaration of consent, which is directed at the bride's father or both sets of parents

Additional readings, prayers or passages you have written

Introduction to the vows

The bride's vows

The groom's vows

Affirmation by guests

Exchange of rings

Blessing of rings

Pronouncement of the union

Recognition of the children (if any)

Prayer of hope or Lord's Prayer (optional)

Special acts of celebration, such as lighting a unity candle or sharing a cup of wine

Benediction and blessing

Presentation of the new couple

ABOVE: *EVERYONE FEELS A PART OF THIS CEREMONY WHEN THE ENTIRE BRIDAL PARTY FACES GUESTS. FLOWERS: FLORAMOR STUDIOS. PHOTO: ELIOT HOLTZMAN*
BELOW: *SCULPTED HEART UNITY CANDLE AND MATCHING TAPERS ON A LARGE BRASS UNITY CANDLE HOLDER. BEVERLY CLARK COLLECTION*

The length of the service can be as long as an hour or as short as just a few minutes. Not surprisingly, the more orthodox the faith, the longer the ceremony usually takes.

Your clergy will want to meet with you and your fiancé several times before your wedding date to go over the wording of your wedding vows. These visits naturally lead to contemplation, as you try to articulate the traits you cherish most about each other and the goals and values you share.

BEYOND WORDS

Symbolism and ritual are an important element of most ceremonies, and you can complement the traditional rites with more recent customs or those borrowed from another culture.

Candlelight ceremonies are particularly magical. They are most effective if held either in the evening or late in the afternoon, with all the lights dimmed. You might place a candle stand, decorated with ribbons and flowers, on either side of the altar, and position other stands at the ends of several rows of pews. A pair of acolytes or ushers can light the candles before the ceremony, or each attendant can carry a candle down the aisle to make a dramatic entrance.

The unity candle, gaining in popularity, is both sweetly symbolic and a good way to include parents in the ceremony. A lit taper candle is placed on each side of the altar, and a single unlit pillar candle is positioned in the center. Once the officiant has pronounced you husband and wife, each of you take your respective candles and, with the flames blending together, light the unity candle. This symbolizes the joining of your lives as one. If parents are to take part, they may bring their own candles and may also read a passage from the Bible or another brief selection before joining you and your groom in lighting the single unity flame.

Sharing a cup of wine is an integral part of the Jewish ceremony, and people of other faiths have adopted this custom, as well. Both bride and groom drink from the same cup, which symbolizes their commitment to share all that the future may bring, and life becomes sweeter because you drink of it together. So, too, life's bitterness is less because you share it.

Along the same lines, sharing a piece of bittersweet chocolate after exchanging vows also makes for a lighthearted moment in the ceremony.

Presenting a rose to each set of parents on your way to the altar is another touching gesture. Together, you and your groom offer a single rose to his parents and then one to yours, uniting the families in this joyous celebration.

"Jumping the broom" is a new-old custom, very popular in African-American weddings. Believed to have originated in the South during the nineteenth century, jumping the broom is as it sounds: the couple jumps over a broom that has been placed on the floor. Several books are now available that describe more customs of African-American weddings, drawing on traditions from this and other countries.

THE PROCESSION

In Europe centuries ago, the journey from hearth to altar was fraught with danger. The bride, and later the couple together, were accompanied by friends who would protect them from animals and robbers, as well as demons (who supposedly loved to feast on a bride and groom's good luck). This custom appeared in nearly every

ABOVE RIGHT: *REPRODUCTION OF QUEEN VICTORIA'S ORIGINAL SILVER LOVING CUP. BEVERLY CLARK COLLECTION. ABOVE: A SYMBOLIC DISPLAY: THE ROMANCE OF DOVES, WHO MATE FOR LIFE, ARE RELEASED FROM BOXES AS THE NEWLYWEDS LEAVE THE CEREMONY. PHOTO: WEDDINGS BY WEINTRAUB*

ABOVE TOP: *Bridesmaids release graceful monarch butterflies from Swallowtail Farms. Photo: Gary C. Varney.* ABOVE: *Specially designed envelopes hold butterflies from The Butterfly Celebration.*

RIGHT: *Elegantly outfitted flower girl prompts the little ring bearer in preparation of their wedding duties. Outfits: LaPetite Affair. Photo: Brian Kramer*

culture, from Germany to China. Borne aloft in a litter, on horseback, in a carriage, or in a simple chair, brides were transported to their weddings without having their feet once touch the ground, where these jealous demons lurked.

Brides and grooms face few threats today other than weather and nerves. The procession now means the walk from one end of the aisle to the other, and varies slightly according to religion and to family circumstances.

In a Christian procession, the groom and best man lead the way, unless they're already waiting at the altar. Next come the ushers, then the bridesmaids, the maid of honor, the ring bearer, the flower girl and, finally, the bride with her father. After the ceremony, the bride and groom return down the aisle followed by the ring bearer and flower girl, the maid of honor with the best man, the bridesmaids and ushers (now paired), and the bride's parents and groom's parents.

Jewish ceremonies differ in that both sets of parents are usually included in the procession. As with Christian weddings, the groom and best man are often waiting at the altar. If they are not, the processional unfolds with the ushers going first, followed by the best man, the groom with his parents, and the remainder of the party as mentioned above. For the recessional, the bride and groom are followed by the bride's parents and the groom's parents, the

CHARMING FLOWER GIRL AND HANDSOME RING BEARER PROCEED DOWN THE HANDPAINTED AISLE RUNNER. PHOTO: FRED MARCUS PHOTOGRAPHY

ABOVE: *An interfaith wedding ceremony. Photo: Durango Steele*

BELOW: *Rabbi and pastor leave the ceremony. Photo: Durango Steele*

RIGHT: *Family medallion necklace used for the combined family ceremonial service incorporates children with a symbolic gesture. Three rings represent the new family union. Beverly Clark Collection*

ring bearer and flower girl, the maid of honor with the best man, and finally the bridesmaids and ushers, who have been paired.

Some couples end their nuptials with the centuries-old European tradition of releasing white doves, a symbol of love, unity, and devotion, into the air as they step outside the church doors. A similar effect can be achieved by releasing dozens of brilliant orange monarch butterflies.

CEREMONIES FOR BLENDED FAMILIES

Many brides and grooms today are blessed with children from a previous marriage. Whether the youngsters are toddlers or high-school seniors, your ceremony can be designed to include them. Even if they are warmly enthusiastic about your union, this is bound to be an emotionally trying time for them, and they'll feel much more secure if they have a specific part to play.

To make the adjustment as easy as possible, you should include the children in the wedding plans from the very beginning. They should not merely be told of your wedding plans, but should be actively involved as participants in the planning, shopping, and decision making. Of course, every situation is different. Some children may choose not to become involved, and this decision should be respected. What's important is to let them know you're thinking of them during this hectic time when they could easily feel neglected.

MUSIC

Music has the power to enthrall, elevate, or evoke a specific time and place. It creates atmosphere and sets the emotional tone of the event. You may choose classical wedding music, or music from an historical era that complements your wedding theme, or special pieces that have a significance for both of you.

The setting will largely determine what sort of music you select for the ceremony. If you're to be married in church, there are few sounds more uplifting than a chorus of human voices accompanied by the church organist. Before making any definite music arrangements or selections, you should check with your church or synagogue to see whether there are any restrictions.

The wedding ceremony calls for four types of music. A prelude is played for the half-hour prior to the ceremony, while your guests are being seated. This may consist of any type of music you like, although I recommend a selection that blends into the background. Just after the mother of the bride is seated, a solo might be sung to let guests know the

ABOVE: *THE MESMERIZING CHORDS OF THE ARISTOCRATIC HARP, PLAYED BY CHRISTINE HOLVICK, COMPLEMENT THE CEREMONY. PHOTO: DURANGO STEELE*

LEFT: *MUSICAL QUARTET ENTERTAINS ON THE GARDEN LAWN. PHOTO: G. GREGORY GEIGER*

T. G. McCary

procession is about to start. The procession usually begins with an instrumental, often a solo, which has a steady, easy-to-walk to beat. Once the attendants have reached the altar, music that announces the bride is played, commanding everyone's attention, as you walk down the aisle. Many brides choose Mendelssohn's classic "Wedding March," from his Midsummer Night's Dream, or Lohengrin's "Bridal Chorus" ("Here Comes the Bride"), but any joyous fanfare is appropriate. One or two songs may be played during the ceremony; any more would be too many. Finally, the recessional music that accompanies the wedding party as they return down the aisle should be triumphant and lively, a rousing climax to this very emotional event.

For smaller weddings, a flautist, guitarist, or small chamber ensemble might provide the ideally graceful notes for your ceremony. Harps and violins are romantic choices, too, but there's nothing that says you can't get a little more creative. Bagpipes make for a rousing procession if they suit the style of your wedding. A trio of trumpet players who provide an unusual fanfare as the bride walks down the aisle might be another choice.

Music also adds to the gaiety during the receiving line. If the ceremony and reception will take place at the same location, you might ask the musicians to remain after the ceremony, playing for another thirty minutes or an hour. If you'll be moving to another site for the reception, you'll need to make arrangements with the band you've hired for the evening.

To get ideas for ceremony music, ask for recommendations and visit the music section of your library. Many music stores now allow customers to listen to CDs before purchasing them. This way you can sample a larger selection than offered at your local library.

PHOTOGRAPHY

A glance at your mother's and grandmother's wedding albums may reveal remarkably similar photos. Frequently, you'll see stiff group portraits, with little spontaneity. While many couples still enjoy having formal portraits taken, the nature of these shots has changed dramatically over the past few years. Photographers today

191

CEREMONY

HEIDI MAURACHER

HEIDI MAURACHER

PHILIPPE CHENG

work with the wedding party to capture the character and emotions of the bride and groom and their families.

Portraits of the bride and groom occupy a category of their own, apart from the rest of the wedding photos. You can have tremendous fun with these, staging ultraromantic vignettes high atop a rocky bluff, on a sand dune or on the balcony of a picturesque inn. The resulting portraits can be as striking as a scene from an epic motion picture or as whimsical as a fairy tale and are a special treat for all.

Wedding portraits are often taken a week or so before the event so that you'll have plenty of time for the photo shoot. If you don't want your groom to see your dress before the big day, you may arrange for a photo session a few weeks later when you return from your honeymoon. It's worth the extra

effort to have such a lovely keepsake of your wedding.

Many photographers now use a photojournalistic approach to shooting the ceremony and reception, trying to capture the various moods of the people as well as the day, collecting candid shots and posed portraits. Be sure your photographer knows who among the crowd is important to you. Ask a close friend to brief the photographer for a few moments prior to the ceremony, or to accompany him or her at the reception for a short time.

Black-and-white photography has made a huge comeback in recent years. Good black-and-white portraits are elegant and romantic, evocative of a more refined era. These can also be hand-tinted, resulting in a nostalgic and quite beautiful effect.

Taking portraits in black and white is an art unto

itself, so it might be worth your while to hire two photographers, one who specializes in the subtle art of black-and-white portraiture, and another who can vividly capture the color and dazzle of the ceremony and reception.

SELECTING A PHOTOGRAPHER

Your wedding photographs will bring you years of pleasure, so select your photographer with great care. Because most good photographers are in demand, start interviewing them six to nine months before your wedding date.

To help put your mind at ease with a personal recommendation, begin by looking through the wedding albums of friends and relatives who live in your area. Your caterer, florist, or reception-site coordinator may also provide some leads. You may want to meet with several photographers before making a final selection. I recommend hiring a professional who specializes in weddings, not a part-time photographer or one who only occasionally handles large events.

When you meet with the photographer, ask to view sample wedding albums. These are perhaps as important as individual shots, since they give you an idea of the scope of the photographer's talent. Discuss formal portraits to be taken either in the photographer's studio or "on location" at various sites.

When interviewing a photographer, be sure to discuss the number of pictures he or she takes, the cost of each print, the style and cost of the albums, and whether there are travel costs or extra fees. Most wedding photographers offer a package, which is a predetermined number of pictures in various sizes for a set fee that includes the prints and the album.

Ordering the package is usually the most cost-effective option. Check to see whether packages are available for parents' albums, too. Most wedding photographers keep the negatives, however. Check to see how long they hold onto these, and whether you can purchase the negatives sometime in the future. Whoever stores the negatives should keep them in a fireproof file.

Last but certainly not least, choose a photographer whose personality will make you and your guests feel at ease. Aside from liking the photographer's work, you should feel confident that the two of you will communicate clearly.

To make sure there are no misunderstandings, include all aspects of your agreement with the photographer in a written contract. The contract should include the wedding date, the photographer's arrival time, length of shooting time, and fees and

ABOVE: *A time for reflection. Photo: Durango Steele*

OPPOSITE: *Photo: Clay Blackmore*

overtime charges, if any. It should also include the photographer's name, so you are guaranteed that the person you met with, and not an assistant, takes the photos. List all locations—the bride's home, ceremony site, and reception site—and provide addresses and directions for each. Include the cost and details of a photo package selection, and the cost of additional photos you may want to order.

If you're planning to send an announcement of your wedding to the newspaper, be sure to inform your photographer so that he can take a black-and-white portrait of the two of you as husband and wife. Order an 8" x 10", black-and-white glossy print to send to the newspaper.

VIDEOTAPING THE WEDDING

Many couples enjoy watching their wedding videotape on their anniversary or sharing it with relatives and friends who were unable to attend. But the most compelling reason to tape your wedding is so that future generations will be able to relive the celebration with you. Imagine if you were able to hear and see your grandparents' wedding day! Now you can make sure your own grandchildren will have that chance.

HANDLING WEDDING PRESSURE

At about the same time you begin to seriously plan your ceremony, you may find that you're losing steam. You've now heard the opinions of many others about your wedding and what would take to make it perfect—a site that's the most romantic, a caterer who's divine, a jazz guitarist who can set just the right mood. You've weathered most of the wedding hurdles: size, the guest list, expense, religious issues, and formality. And you may have learned the hard way that heated debates can erupt over such seemingly simple things as wineglasses and bath towels.

The months before a wedding are extremely stressful, and you'll need a sense of humor to survive them. This is especially true in the final six weeks before the big day. Compromise where necessary, try to maintain a rational perspective, and be considerate of your future husband's feelings. I recommend taking a breather if it's at all possible. Escape may ease the pressure, even if it's only for a night or an afternoon.

RECEPTIONS

THE WEDDING RECEPTION continues to be a celebration of good fortune, just as it's been since earliest times, when an elaborate feast was presented in the town square and the entire village partied for days on end. Ancient societies cheered a marriage because it meant combined wealth and more children—an overall increase in the worth of the tribe. Nowadays, the good luck has very little to do with property and everything to do with love.

In a way, a wedding reception is like a valentine gift to your family and friends, whose love and support you've had the great fortune to enjoy. To thank them, and to celebrate the fate that brought you and your fiancé together, you want to put on an unforgettable party. That doesn't necessarily mean the most lavish event ever, but rather one

that serves up an effervescent mix of diversion, delicious food, raucous revelry, and quiet moments for reflection.

Sometimes, after the wedding has come and gone and a couple are looking over their photo album, they'll marvel at the details, the grandeur, or the intimate beauty of the whole event. Their own memories of that day may be a dreamlike blur of excitement and emotion. Only when looking again at the delighted faces of their

PREVIOUS PAGE: *PLAZA HOTEL, NEW YORK RECEPTION.*
PHOTO: FRED MARCUS PHOTOGRAPHY
TABLE SETTING BY FLORAMOR. PHOTO: ELIOT HOLTZMAN

200

A Southern Extravaganza

The lavish wedding of Charlotte Ann Hall and Greg O'Neal took place at 7:30 p.m. at the Cathedral of St. Philip in Atlanta. A full Episcopalian mass for more than a thousand guests preceded an elaborate reception in the Grand Ballroom of the Georgian Terrace, downtown. Guests enjoyed a magnificent buffet that was highlighted by white linen covered tables and vibrant floral arrangements by Carithers Flower Shop. The Cecil Welch orchestra entertained throughout the evening.

THIS PAGE AND OPPOSITE:
PHOTOS: KEVIN HYDE

THE ROOM TOOK ON AN ENCHANTED AIR WITH GOLDEN STARS PROJECTED ON THE WALLS, VIA PINLIGHTS. THE SEVEN-TIERED WEDDING CAKE REVEALED A HEAVENLY SURPRISE WITH EACH LAYER PRODUCED IN A DIFFERENT FLAVORED CHEESECAKE, BY CLASSIC CHEESECAKES. THE CUSTOM-CARVED ICE SCULPTURE REPRESENTED ST. BASILS IN MOSCOW, A COMMEMORATION OF A COLLEGE ADVENTURE. VARIOUS VODKA FLAVORS, POURED FROM THE TOP OF THE SCULPTURE, SWIRLED DOWN THROUGH, AND ENDED AS A CHILLED SHOT IN A WAITING GLASS BELOW.

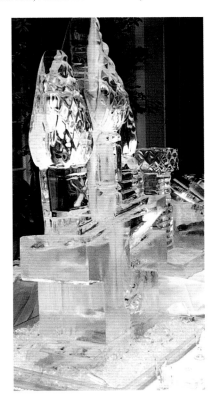

guests can they begin to get a sense of the party they hosted. The happiness everyone shares at the reception makes all the months of planning worthwhile.

TYPES OF RECEPTIONS

A casual afternoon tea party, or a formal dinner dance in a grand ballroom atop one of the city's skyscrapers? The style of reception you choose is a matter of taste and budget. Once you've determined the time of your ceremony and finalized the guest list, you can decide what type of reception will work best for you. It can take place at any time of day, depending on the religious restrictions that might apply to your ceremony.

A breakfast or brunch reception is pleasantly appropriate following a morning ceremony at nine or ten o'clock. A breakfast buffet typically includes an assortment of fresh fruit, croissants, rolls and quiches, cold cuts, and cheeses. With a sit-down breakfast, you might start with fresh juice and fruit, then serve an omelet or eggs Benedict. Whether your feast is sit-down or buffet style, you'll likely want to cap the morning with wedding cake and a champagne toast. Other alcoholic beverages are optional at breakfast (naturally, you'll provide coffee, tea, and juice). For couples who want to keep the expense of alcoholic beverages down, a breakfast reception is a good choice.

Luncheon receptions are similar to brunch receptions and may be either sit-down or buffet style. They generally follow a late morning or "high" noon ceremony and are served between twelve and two o'clock in the afternoon. Buffet luncheons may include a variety of salads, followed by an entrée such as poached salmon or shrimp. Chicken or pasta, both very popular, are a delicious and less expensive alternative.

At a sit-down lunch, the guests are often treated to champagne, cocktails, and hors d'oeuvres while they make their way through the receiving line. Once they're seated, a white wine may be served with soup or salad. The choice of entrée is limited only by your budget and your caterer's imagination, but in general luncheon fare is lighter than a dinner menu. As with breakfast, the meal will be topped off with wedding cake, served with coffee and tea. Having an espresso/cappuccino bar or offering chocolate cups filled with cordials adds a nice touch. So, too, does a second champagne toast.

Tea receptions are lovely and can be relatively inexpensive to host, and are perfect for couples trying to accommodate a large guest list on a small budget. Tea receptions may be held in a home or garden, and since they feature finger foods rather than full meals, rented tables and chairs are not necessary. Tea receptions can be wonderfully festive

occasions because people love to nibble on sandwiches, fresh fruit, and wedding cake, and the relaxed atmosphere suits some couples better than a more formal affair. The tea reception is generally held between two and five o'clock in the afternoon. Coffee and tea or punch, with or without champagne or wine, may be served.

Cocktail receptions, held between four o'clock and seven-thirty, have many of the same advantages as tea receptions: they can be held in any location, including your home, and rentals are usually minimal. The big difference, of course, is that many cocktail receptions feature an open bar and alcohol can be costly. This type of reception is, however, still less expensive than one that includes a full meal. Most hosts will offer guests a variety of hot and cold hors d'oeuvres, followed by wedding cake. Champagne, wine,

punch, and beer are usually offered, and coffee and tea should be served as well.

A dinner reception usually begins between six and eight o'clock in the evening. In many cases, cocktails and hors d'oeuvres are served in the first hour, with a sit-down or buffet dinner following. A cocktail hour of some kind gives people time to go through the receiving line and mingle with friends, especially when a sit-down dinner follows. If you need to keep expenses down, offer wine and beer rather than a full bar.

Seated receptions usually feel more formal than buffet-style dinners. A seated reception gives the hosts more control: it's easier to get your guests' attention when the traditional events, such as cutting the cake, begin. Some people feel that a sit-down service tends to quiet a party and discourages people from mingling.

ABOVE: *Delectable cheese, vegetable and assorted dips are presented on this garden buffet table.*
PHOTO: *Jennifer Drake*
LEFT: *Lemons make an attractive option to support roses, delphiniums and stocks in this clear glass vase.* PHOTO: *Durango Steele*
RIGHT: *An abounding mixed-flower centerpiece is softly lit by a tiny silver candle lamp.*
PHOTO: *G. Gregory Geiger*

PREVIOUS PAGE: *Roving minstrel adds musical amusement to this cozy patio reception.*
PHOTO: *Durango Steele*

At a buffet reception, the hosts decide whether guests will have assigned seats or will choose their own seating. Be sure to plan the event so that your guests don't have to wait in a long line to get their food. If you have invited two hundred guests or more, consider setting up two buffet tables, one at each end of the room.

Food-station receptions have become very popular in recent years. The stations, small buffet tables set up around the room or garden, feature different types of cuisine, such as seafood, bread and cheeses, roast beef, and so forth. The gaily decorated tables encourage guests to sample all the delicacies at their leisure, rather than filling their plates at a single visit. Guests are more likely to mingle, while they are waiting at the various stations. For a bit of casual entertainment, have the servers create the cuisine in front of the guests. Having servers dish out won tons straight from the wok, crêpes from the pan, or sushi from the cutting board, adds a festive element.

BELOW: *A SPOT IN THE SHADE IS SELECTED FOR THIS GARDEN BUFFET TABLE.*
PHOTO: DURANGO STEELE

PLANNING THE RECEPTION

You'll begin the nitty-gritty planning of the reception by considering what the site has to offer in the way of size, facilities, and ambiance. Some hotel and country club sites are accustomed to staging weddings and will assign you an on-staff wedding coordinator who can recommend florists, musicians, or photographers and help coordinate the other details of the event. Most brides confer frequently with the wedding coordinator, reviewing the menu and making sure things are moving along smoothly.

The challenge in hotel or country club weddings is to make them uniquely your own. The wedding coordinator should be enthusiastic about your vision of the event, and forthcoming about any trouble spots he or she might perceive in your plan. If you're

ABOVE: *Shimmering strings of lights illuminate this enormous tent. Photo: G. Gregory Geiger*

BELOW LEFT: *The Master Chef in his outdoor creative kitchen. Photo: Durango Steele*

BELOW RIGHT: *Wine servers prepare to pour the all-important champagne. Photo: Durango Steele*

PREVIOUS PAGE RIGHT: *Pedestal arrangements with colorful deep blue and lavender delphiniums mixed with anthuriums*

and roses border this patio for the wedding ceremony. Flowers: Hearts Bloom. Photo: Mark Papay

Putting the plan on paper.

Photo: Durango Steele

working with a florist or other designer who's not familiar with the hotel's way of doing things, you should include the wedding coordinator in all the important meetings.

Weddings that take place in less traditional locations or at home still need the watchful eye of a coordinator—a role usually filled by the bride and her mother or by a professional wedding consultant. More grooms are getting involved in the planning these days, too, which can be a great help.

The basic elements of the reception are the decorations, catering, and music. The physical comfort of the place is another element to bear in mind. If your wedding will be held outdoors, the possibility of rain, wind, humidity, or heat must be factored in, and you'll need to have a backup plan in case of inclement weather. Indoor venues need to be checked to make sure they have adequate heating or air-conditioning, changing rooms for the wedding party, restrooms, and kitchen facilities. Almost any site can be made to work with the help of an additional tent or two, but those come at a cost.

MARK PAPAS: CHAIR DECOR: HARTS BLOOM

DECORATIONS

To a large extent, decor at a wedding means flowers, but most florists today do much more than just arrange blossoms and foliage. Many can also supply lighting, design tables from the cloth to the napkin rings, build structures, and offer you a wide selection of props. Florists work closely with caterers to arrange artful buffets, and they'll design the cake table to perfectly complement your wedding cake. In fact, many cakes these days feature real flowers as well as sugar ones.

Even if the reception will take place at a different site than the ceremony, there should be some continuity in the flowers used at each location. Should the architecture of the sites be quite different—say, a baroque church and a modern ballroom—the flowers will create a visual bridge between the two, helping to maintain a single spirit throughout the wedding. Often large floral arrangements can be used at both the ceremony and the reception. Altar displays, for example, can later be used to grace the wedding cake or the buffet table

Photo Andrea Laurita Custom Florist

Brian Kramer

207

or to flank the bandstand, depending on their size. I've attended weddings where topiaries that served as pew decorations did double duty as centerpieces. A creative florist will tell you all the ways you can get the most out of the flowers you purchase.

In addition to flowers, receptions may boast other visual elements that add to the room's elegance or whimsy. Potted plants and trees are commonly used to soften a room's hard edges, cut down on the noise level, or cordon off areas. Twinkle lights are becoming a staple at weddings, and if the tone isn't overly formal, balloons and streamers can add loads of atmosphere at relatively little cost.

According to Laura Little of Floramor Studios in San Francisco, lighting is a close second to flowers when it comes to decorating a reception. "Weddings are getting very elaborate these days, and many brides are willing to spend a few extra dollars to spotlight their tables and centerpieces or project patterns onto the dance floor. Lighting really enhances the atmosphere."

The right lighting can utterly transform a room. At one recent wedding, panels of

ABOVE: *PASTEL PINK DRAPED FABRIC AND FLORAL TREATMENT TRANSFORMS AND SOFTENS THIS TENT SETTING. PHOTO: CLAY BLACKMORE*

OPPOSITE: *WROUGHT-IRON CANDELABRAS DECORATED WITH ROSES, MAPLE LEAVES AND GRAPES BY CLARE WEBBER COMPLEMENT LOVELY DEEP PINK DAMASK TABLECLOTHS FOR THIS RECEPTION. SALAD PLATES ARE GARNISHED WITH WHITE ROSE BUDS AND PETALS FOR THAT EXTRA SPECIAL TOUCH. PHOTO: G. GREGORY GEIGER*

sheer white fabric flanked by curtains were hung at various points along the walls. A lovely image of a fountain under a lattice archway, with soft greenery in the background, was projected onto the panels. The view through these large "garden windows" gave guests a light, summery, garden feeling, even though the wedding took place indoors.

Another delightful lighting trick is to project stars or other patterns onto the walls, ceiling, or floor of the room. At the 1940s-style jazz wedding of Ryan Patterson and Richard Plotkin, old newsreels were projected onto one wall. The flickering black-and-white footage helped bring the era to life and added another dimension to the party.

Lately, there has been a resurgence of color in wedding decoration. Ivory and peach palettes are classics, but today's brides sometimes opt for more intense shades. Primary colors can be overwhelming in a large room; table after table of bright reds, oranges, and purples is hard on the eyes. Instead, think Renaissance hues—rich jewel tones such as coral, deep rose, violet, burgundy, and amber gold.

THE RECEPTION AS A CANVAS

The florist or wedding designer's mission is either to turn a ho-hum room into something remarkable or to tastefully complement a room that's outstanding in its own right, as is the case with many grand hotels or historic mansions.

An anonymous room is a blank canvas for the innovative designer. Floramor's Laura Little notes that in these rooms the first priority is to make the perimeter recede and to focus attention on the tables, dance floor, and centerpieces. Bring in tall ficus trees and place them throughout the room to form a leafy rooftop over the tables. With the overhead lights off and twinkle lights sparkling in the trees, the ceiling vanishes and the room takes on a magical feeling. Candles on the tables warm the

scene and draw attention to the tabletops and centerpieces. Patterns projected onto the dance floor add another point of interest. Fragrance is important as well; aromatic flowers imbue the room with a subtle, romantic ambiance.

For one recent wedding, Floramor transformed a large, bland room into the perfect setting for a gypsy festival. Each table was draped in a different intense color, then overdraped with a sheer black cloth that glittered with gold and silver stars. Centerpieces were tall vases featuring lush flower arrangements that matched the tablecloth color. A fog machine provided even more atmosphere, with the fog lit by blue and purple lights.

The gypsy theme didn't stop at decorations. A troupe of gypsy musicians played during dinner (later on a dance band took over), and exotically-garbed

fortune-tellers entertained the guests. Six brightly colored tents—turquoise with black polka dots, and green-and-black striped—were set up around the room. In each sat a soothsayer to read palms, tarot cards, or tea leaves. Throughout the evening guests were free to roam from tent to tent, exploring their futures. All this in a room that, by day, was a humble meeting hall.

ABOVE: *RICHLY-PATTERNED DESIGN IS PROJECTED ONTO THIS BALLROOM DANCE FLOOR. PHOTO: FRED MARCUS PHOTOGRAPHY.* RIGHT: *IMPECCABLE DRAPING AND ARISTOCRATIC CANDELABRAS WITH TOWERING FLOWER ARRANGEMENTS PROMOTE THE MAGIC OF THE OCCASION. PHOTO: G. GREGORY GEIGER*
OPPOSITE: *THIS HEAVENLY CLEAR TENT SHIMMERS WITH HUNDREDS OF TWINKLE LIGHTS WHILE GUESTS ENJOY THE SOFT FLICKERING LIGHT OF TABLE CANDLES. PHOTO: MONTE CLAY*

DECORATING GRAND ROOMS

Rooms that are already decorated present a different challenge for the wedding designer. Here, the first decision is whether to work with the existing design and palette or to work around them. If a room has beautiful windows and detailing but less-than-delightful colors, Laura Little suggests choosing a neutral palette that will make the colors less noticeable. Monochromatic flowers in shades of blush, ivory, and peach work well, especially if the arrangements are striking. Use a mix of large and small blossoms, lots of texture, interesting greenery, even twigs and branches. Fruit can

make a monochromatic display more interesting: golden pears, red pomegranates, and rust crab apples all add variety and depth to the decoration.

In a room that is beautifully decorated, you'll want to carry through the existing colors and style of decor. In San Francisco's Sheraton Palace, Floramor was called upon to decorate an ornate, French-style ballroom for a reception that would host 450 guests. The goals were to dress up an already elaborate room and create an intimate atmosphere.

The colors of the carpet, dusty shades of pink, coral, cream, and butterscotch, provided a point of departure. These hues were repeated in centerpieces of garden roses, peonies, orchids, hydrangea, and Japanese weeping birch. The blossoms cascaded down from custom-designed, five-foot candelabras that matched the ornate spirit of the room. Table linens were gold

and coral, and a small rose was slipped into the French ribbon that tied each napkin. A pattern of garden roses in the same warm shades was projected onto the dance floor. Everywhere the colors of the carpet were reflected in the design, so that the room seemed all of a single piece. The dusky hues also helped cozy the large space.

The keys to decorating an exquisite room are to augment the existing style, mirroring the colors whenever possible. Bear this in mind when you're looking at sites: either be flexible about the colors you want, or choose a location that will work with the palette you have your heart set on.

FOOD, GLORIOUS FOOD

The food and beverage portion of the wedding usually carries the greatest expense, so review your options very carefully. When your reception is being held in a home, garden, or hall that allows you to hire your own caterer, your choices are numerous. Good caterers, like talented florists and photographers, are booked months in advance. Start interviewing them at least six months before the wedding, and be prepared to leave a deposit in order to reserve your date and time.

FLOWERS: HEARTS BLOOM. PHOTOS: DURANGO STEELE

When interviewing caterers, find out what services they provide. Some handle only food preparation, delivery, and service, while others coordinate all the details of the reception, including food preparation and serving, equipment rental, setup and cleanup, liquor, and other beverages, bartenders, flowers, and other decorations. If a caterer doesn't provide all these services, he or she will probably know of reputable people you can contact directly.

Most caterers have photographs of weddings they have done. Scrutinize the artistry with which the food is displayed, and

ask the caterer whether the crew set up the displays themselves or whether a florist helped. Before hiring a caterer with whom you're unfamiliar, it's a good idea to check references and, if possible, taste the food before signing a contract. You may not get to sample your particular menu before you sign, but you might be able to do so a few weeks prior to the wedding. You may very well spend thousands of dollars on your wedding feast, so the quality of the meal should thrill you.

DELICIOUS FOOD AND CREATIVELY PRESENTED MENU. PHOTOS: DURANGO STEELE.

BOUNTIFUL BREAD DISPLAYED IN BASKETS. PHOTO: JENNIFER DRAKE

ICE SCULPTURE HOLDS FRESH SEAFOOD. PHOTO: G. GREGORY GEIGER

DURANGO STEELE

Read the caterer's contract carefully to be sure it includes everything you agreed on and states the total price; don't forget to check the cancellation policies. Caterers charge either a flat fee based on the number of guests or a fee per person. A 15 percent service charge, plus sales tax, is usually added to the total. Most caterers require a deposit of 50 to 75 percent, along with a total guest count, a week or two before the ceremony. The balance is usually paid immediately after the reception.

DECIDING ON THE MENU

Your caterer will suggest menus that fit the style and budget of your wedding. A good caterer is flexible, will listen to your opinions and inquire about your preferences. The challenge is to create a menu that's interesting without being extreme. There will likely be at least three generations at your wedding, and they may have somewhat different tastes. If you choose a conventional entrée such as chicken, your caterer should suggest less typical side dishes, sauces, or salads that will make the meal stand out from the ordinary.

Another way to make the wedding feast unique is to include food that has special meaning for you and your groom. Perhaps there's a type of bread his family shared at every holiday meal, or a delicacy your beloved cousin was famous for. Bring the caterer the recipes, and be sure these items are included in the tasting prior to your wedding day.

RIGHT: *Rustic willow basket holds bread. Photo: Durango Steele*

BELOW: *Stylish copper pots and lilacs are in place to decorate this pasta bar.*

Photo: G. Gregory Geiger.

HOTEL CATERING

Because weddings are a large source of income for most hotels, their catering departments work hard to keep wedding patrons happy. While they'll offer you a selection of set menus, they are usually very flexible when it comes to augmenting or changing the standard fare. The hotel chef will probably be glad to make any recipe you like, but most hotels will not allow you to bring in food of your own.

When you and your fiancé have decided on a menu, try to arrange a tasting with the hotel a few weeks prior to the wedding, possibly a lunch with the chef in the kitchen. This is your opportunity to fine-tune the menu and make last-minute changes. You won't get a chance to taste the cake, however.

ABOVE: *A TOAST OF GOOD LUCK TO THE NEWLYWEDS! GUESTS ENJOYED A FUN-FILLED OUTDOOR GARDEN RECEPTION.*

PHOTO: DURANGO STEELE

BELOW: *SERVERS SET UP THE BAR AS THEY AWAIT THE WEDDING PARTYGOERS.*

PHOTO: DURANGO STEELE

KEN COHEN, OWNER OF THE CAPPUCCINO CONNECTION, SERVES THE BRIDE AND GROOM THEIR FAVORITES. PHOTO: DURANGO STEELE

DRINK AND BE MERRY

Wedding feasts mean wedding toasts—the more, the happier. Unless yours will be a totally nonalcoholic affair, you will certainly want to supply enough champagne for a toast or two. Although liquor can add substantially to the cost of the reception, there are a number of ways to control those costs without dampening the spirit of the party. As you're reviewing your options, keep in mind that most people drink more at nighttime and during warm weather. The average person consumes three or four drinks an evening, or approximately one every hour.

If your reception will take place in a hotel, restaurant or club, check the type of alcohol the venue supplies and the cost per drink. You may want to host an unlimited open bar for the entire time or limit it to a cocktail hour, then serve wine with dinner, followed by coffee and after-dinner drinks. Or, you may simply serve champagne for toasting and nonalcoholic drinks for the rest of the evening. Whether or not you're providing alcohol, have a selection of beverages such as iced tea, sparkling cider, mineral water, or punch on hand for guests who don't drink spirits.

Some hotels and restaurants let you provide your own wine or champagne. If so, they'll usually charge a separate corkage fee per bottle. Some locations also charge extra to pour coffee. If you're having your wedding at a venue that doesn't supply alcoholic beverages, you can either purchase them yourself or leave it to your caterer. As always, you'll save some money by doing it yourself, but you may not be able to return extra bottles. If a caterer provides the drinks, you'll pay only for bottles that are opened.

SPECIAL TOUCHES

A few well-placed props can enliven your reception and inspire your guests. Here are some suggestions:

Place small bottles of blowing bubbles at each guest's place. Decorate them or personalize the labels with the names of the bride and groom and the wedding date. Bubbles can fill the air as the bride and groom have their first dance. Or, you might replace the tradition of rice-throwing with bubble-blowing.

Place a disposable camera on each table, with a note asking guests to take pictures during the reception. It's fun for the guests, and it guarantees some great candid shots. Assign someone to collect all the cameras at the end of the reception. Naturally, these candid shots should not replace professional photography!

On the back of your wedding invitation or on a separate enclosure, print a request that each guest share a favorite memory of the bride or groom. Instruct guests to write this memory on a piece of paper, sign it, and bring it to the reception, where the papers will be collected and later put in a memory book. If yours will be a smaller, more intimate reception, consider asking guests to read their memory aloud so everyone might savor it.

ABOVE: *Personalized wine bottle, flower girl blowing bubbles and monogrammed heart cookies. Photos: Durango Steele. Intricately detailed silverplated Picture Frame Placecards™, Beverly Clark Collection. Gift totes filled with sea shells to make picture frames keep children occupied and provide a memorable keepsake. Children's table designed by Hearts Bloom. Photo: Mark Papay*

RITUALS OF THE RECEPTION

The reception usually begins with a receiving line, a lovely way to greet guests and thank them for sharing your special day. If the guests are small in number, you may want to greet them immediately after the ceremony rather than waiting for them to arrive at the reception site.

Should there be a receiving line at the reception, try to select the site for it ahead of time. Choose a location that avoids congestion. Keep the conversation short— you don't want your guests standing in line too long. This is a good time to invite people to sign the guest book, which may be placed either before or after the line.

Your mother usually heads the line; your father may stand beside her or circulate among the guests. The decision of who stands in the line is yours. However, the best man, ushers, flower girl, and ring bearer normally do not participate. To help the receiving line move more quickly, it may be necessary to exclude the maid of honor and bridesmaids.

A schedule is a good idea for yourself, the caterer, the musicians, and the photographer, to help maintain a smooth flow of events. It's especially necessary when you have a time limit on the location, which may need to include setup and cleanup time. Extra charges will be applied, should you run overtime.

Most receptions last three to five hours. If not taken earlier, wedding pictures are taken in the first half-hour after the ceremony. Guests begin to arrive, mingle, and drink as the musicians begin to play. Soon the receiving line forms, and the wedding party greets the guests, who are nibbling on refreshments.

In the second hour, the buffet is announced or the guests are seated for dinner. Reception seating depends on the type and formality of the reception and on the layout of the room. Position the bride's table in a central location. The bridal table may include the bride and groom and their parents, or the bride and groom and the attendants, or both.

During this time, the best man proposes the first toast, after everyone has been served a toasting beverage. Champagne is traditional, but white wine or punch is often served. The bride and groom do not stand or drink when they are being toasted. Others may want to propose a toast as well, but it's best to limit the number to two or three. The groom may then toast his bride, his parents, and his new in-laws. Following this, any congratulatory telegrams are read by the best man. After the toasts, the newlyweds share a first dance, allowing the rest of the guests to dance as well. Just before or immediately after the main course, the band leader or master of ceremonies will signal the beginning of the dancing formalities.

MUSIC

The music you choose for the reception will set the tone for the entire evening. Just as with the menu, the challenge here is to arrange a music selection that is enjoyable to all without being bland or tedious. Couples generally choose soft music during the first hour, as background for the receiving line or cocktail gathering. Later on, after the meal, the musicians will pick up the tempo and play more danceable tunes. Your reception may feature a solo pianist, a small combo of mixed instruments, or a larger orchestra from eight to twenty people. Instead of dance music, some couples opt for an acoustic guitarist or a string quartet to accompany the wedding repast.

Keep in mind the varying ages of your guests when selecting your music and look for musicians who can play a wide range of songs. You'll want to review the timing of important announcements, such as the grand entrance, the first dance, the cake-cutting, and the throwing of the tossing bouquet and garter, with the bandleader.

Most bands today have presentation videos, but try to hear them live. You'll get a sense of the kind of energy they can generate.

RECORDED MUSIC

Recorded music is more popular today than ever before, not only because the equipment has become so much more sophisticated, but also the cost is considerably less than a live band. Variety is virtually unlimited and space requirements are minimal. Your disc jockey might act as a Master of Ceremonies, as well.

Whatever your choice, make your musical arrangements as far in advance as possible. Good references, a creative and varied playlist, and a written contract are in order.

OPPOSITE: *Violinists lined the staircase as guests arrived at the wedding of Allyson Brooke Newman and Jay Adam Sachs. Photo: John Reilly*
CENTER: *The Gene Donati orchestra entertained guests at the dinner reception of Connie Goodman and David Litman, held at the Lord Baltimore Hotel, Baltimore, MD. Cream and blush colortones, with touches of gold graced this Palace-of-Versaille-style reception. Crystal and gold candelabras adorned with roses and lilies graced the custom-made ivory damask tablecloths. Photo: Monte Clay.* BELOW: *Photo: Durango Steele*

225

THE FINE ART OF ASSIGNED SEATING

As any experienced hostess knows, there's a skill to mixing and matching guests at a party. If you plan on assigning seats, be sure to ask someone from the groom's family to join in the task. Try to seat people at a table where they will know at least one person or have similar interests with the others. Older people often have difficulty hearing and might do best seated in a relatively quiet area, away from the music. Young children should sit with their parents or at a designated children's table, with activities and perhaps someone assigned to watch them. Use your discretion when it comes to teenagers; seat them with parents or place them at a table together.

Assigned seating opens the door for a number of clever ideas in place cards that can double as favors. Here are a few:

Give each guest a small porcelain bell with the bride's and groom's name on the outside and the guest's table number painted on the inside.

Have each guest's name engraved on a wine or champagne glass. Place the glasses on the tables to serve as place cards. Guests must then find their own glasses before sitting. The glass is the guest's to keep.

OPPOSITE: *BEAUTIFULLY APPOINTED BRIDE AND GROOM'S TABLE IS ADORNED WITH CANDLES AND FLOWER ARRANGEMENTS MATCHING THOSE ON THE DRAMATIC FIREPLACE.*
FLOWERS: SCOTT HOGUE
PHOTO: DURANGO STEELE

LEFT: *A MAJESTIC JEWISH TRADITIONAL DANCE TO CELEBRATE THE MARRIED COUPLE.*
PHOTO: JOANN PECORARO
BELOW: *BRIDE AND GROOM DANCE TO THE DELIGHT OF FAMILY AND FRIENDS.*
PHOTO: MONTE CLAY

At a number of specialty chocolate shops, you can have your guests' names molded in chocolate—a big hit with chocolate lovers!

Use a small picture frame to act as both place card and wedding favor. Write the guest's name in calligraphy on a small piece of paper, slide it into the frame, and place the frame at the appropriate setting.

If the reception is large, with open seating or standing, you may choose to allow guests to dance after they go through the receiving line. This gives them something to do while you finish greeting guests and catch your breath. The dance floor can then be cleared so that all eyes will be focused on the newlyweds when they begin their first dance as husband and wife.

The cake should be cut no later than three and a half hours into the reception. Everyone—especially children—looks forward to this with great anticipation, so you might like to schedule it even earlier than the three-and-a-half-hour mark. You don't want people to leave and miss this festive event. At a luncheon or dinner reception, cut the cake just before or during the coffee service. At an afternoon tea or cocktail reception, cut the cake after everyone has passed through the receiving line and has been served drinks.

The bandleader or master of ceremonies announces that the cake is about to be cut. The groom places his right hand over yours, and together you cut the first slice. You then offer each other a bite, which signifies your willingness to share life together. Next, the bride offers a piece of cake to her new in-laws, and the groom might do the same. The rest of the cake is then cut and served to the guests.

In the final half-hour of the reception, the bride tosses her bouquet and the groom throws the garter. Bride and groom then make their getaway amid hails of rice, birdseed, or flower petals, or enveloped in a shower of bubbles blown by the guests.

LEFT: *This happy groom renders the traditional garter toss to eager singles. Photo: Scott A. Nelson*

BELOW: *Bridesmaids and guests attempt to catch the bride's bouquet in hopes that they might become the next to marry. Photo: Durango Steele.*

OPPOSITE: *A shower of good luck rose petals on the departing bride and groom. Photo: Clay Blackmore*

$\mathscr{C}$AKES

$\mathbf{W}$HEN THE BRIDE AND GROOM step up to slice the first piece of wedding cake, an excited hush falls across the assembled guests. The cake is the crown jewel of the wedding feast. Next to you and your groom, it's the centerpiece of the wedding. Your cake may be a traditional creamy white, adorned with ribbons of pale frosting and exquisite sugar blossoms, or a chocolate extravaganza boasting a cascade of fresh yellow roses. Some cakes are as ornate as a French chandelier, while others are astonishing works of modern sculpture. Decorations can include everything from edible gold leaf to tiny, perfect marzipan fruits. The only limit is your imagination.

Today's sumptuous wedding cakes are the distant descendants of an ancient Roman ritual. Wedding guests would pelt the bride and groom with grains of wheat to encourage a fertile union. Eventually, bakers made small wedding cakes of wheat that the groom would break above the head of his bride, letting guests nibble the fallen crumbs, sharing in the newlywed's good fortune. During the Middle Ages, sweet buns replaced the wheat cakes. In England, wedding guests would pile these buns into a tall pyramid and urge the bride and groom to kiss over the top of the stack. A French baker, who witnessed the spectacle, decided the wedding pyramid needed sugar frosting, and thus was born the first multilayered wedding cake. The French croquembouche, a tower of pastry puffs iced with fine sugar frosting, is still served at many weddings.

Until the eighteenth century, wedding cakes were usually dense, dark fruitcakes. With the introduction of refined flour, they evolved into the fanciful architectural masterworks we delight in today. The fruitcake was relegated to the position of groom's cake, a piece of which is traditionally sent home with each guest. According to wedding lore, a single woman who tucks a slice of groom's cake beneath her pillow the night of the wedding will see her future husband in her dreams.

CAKE DESIGNS

Wedding cake bakers consider themselves artists, and you'll be dazzled by the choices available and the sophistication of their designs. Your wedding cake should be harmonious with the overall style of the wedding. The season has an impact, too. Cakes at outdoor summer weddings may feature basket-weave frosting and dozens of fresh flowers, while more formal, indoor affairs may call

PREVIOUS PAGE: *INTRICATE ICING OF HAND PIPED PALE, CAFE AU LAIT BUTTER CREAM FROSTING AND EXQUISITELY EMBELLISHED FLORAL SWAGS, INTERTWINED WITH RIBBONS AND BOWS DECORATE THE CAKE. GOLD BRUSHED PEARS, GREEN GRAPES AND ROSES SET OFF THE CAKE TABLE. CAKE: FANTASY FROSTING. PHOTO: AMEDEO, COURTESY OF FLOWERS& MAGAZINE.* RIGHT: *THE NEW MR. AND MRS. JAY ADAM SACHS ARE ALL SMILES AS THEY CUT INTO THIS SIX-TIERED CAKE BY SYLVIA WEINSTOCK. EXQUISITELY ADORNED WITH DELICATE SUGAR FLOWERS, COLORS MATCH THE COUPLE'S CEREMONY AND RECEPTION. PHOTO: JOHN REILLY*

LEFT: *Delicate white fondant of pressed lace set over yellow fondant and decorated with gum paste sugar roses, tulips, sweet peas, primroses and ranunculas. The sugar vase of flowers becomes the bride's keepsake.*
CAKE: *Rosemary Watson of Sugar Bouquets.*
BELOW: *Garlands of beautiful sugar flowers and ribbons are added to pressed lace made of fondant and candy clay, set on a butter cream base. Award-winning design by Rosemary Watson of Sugar Bouquets.*

OPPOSITE RIGHT: *Scalloped lace of sugar resembles lace doilies.*
CAKE: *Jan Kish. Photo: Lambert Photographs*
BOTTOM: *Smaller heart-shaped cake of intricately sculpted sugar scalloped edging. Cake: Jan Kish. Photo: Lambert Photographs*
FAR RIGHT: *Grape-embossed motif and peach-colored white chocolate roses are accented with fresh flowers and herbs. Cake: Cakework. Photo: Peter Diggs*

for a multitiered cake with intricate pleats, piping, and volumes of delicate sugar ribbons and blooms. The cake may be any shape you please: round, square, diamond, or even heart-shaped. Tiers may be separated by columns or stacked directly on top of one another.

The cake itself is no longer limited to white or yellow. Instead, couples ask bakers to devise recipes that will please all tastes. Today, it's common for each tier of the cake to be a different flavor. Carrot, hazelnut, orange, mocha, and chocolate are a few favorites.

Rosemary Watson of Sugar Bouquets in Morristown, New Jersey, has created a popular four-layer cake that is a good example of the variety available to brides and grooms today. It features sour-cream chocolate cake on the top and bottom layers, with two inside layers of white or orange cake, flecked with semisweet chocolate confetti. The fillings that separate the layers may be raspberry, orange grand marnier, hazelnut butter cream, or a host of other options. The entire cake is underfrosted with chocolate *ganache* to seal in moisture and cut the sweetness of the outer frosting. Watson's cakes are adorned with the sugar flowers for which she's become famous, but she has also decorated cakes with molded violins, pianos, musical notes, even ladybugs, always hidden among the flowers to keep the effect subtle.

Watson designs her cakes to look just as good sliced and on the plate as they do on the cake table. "You want all those people who are counting calories to eat the cake," she laughs. "It has to look so good that they can't pass it up."

Jan Kish, proprietor and cake wizard at Jan Kish–La Petite Fleur, in Columbus, Ohio, specializes in cakes frosted with rolled fondant, an icing with an alabaster-smooth finish. "It provides a canvas for the cake designer," she says. That canvas is often a colorful one. Kish has created red, royal blue, hunter green, and antique white cakes. One cake of which she is particularly proud featured a cascading bow, designed to match the one on the bride's gown, tumbling down the

tiers. Another cake was fashioned to resemble a porcelain fruit basket overflowing with flowers.

FRESH FLOWERS OR SUGAR FLOWERS

Some wedding cakes boast intricate geometric patterns; Art Deco flourishes, or bas-relief scenes that resemble Wedgwood porcelain. But most cakes are embellished with flowers—either exquisite sugar concoctions or fresh blossoms that look delectable enough to eat. Fresh flowers began to appear on wedding cakes several years ago. Prior to that, cakes featured only sugar blossoms. Today, most bakers are able to design artful cakes with either fresh or sugar flowers.

Whether or not the wedding cake itself has fresh flowers, the cake table is usually decorated with a floral display. When deciding which flowers to use on the cake table, bear in mind that you don't want the flowers to draw attention away from the cake. For that reason, if your cake is white or a light color, don't decorate the table with bright flowers. Greenery and a few tasteful blossoms will create a more effective backdrop for the cake.

OPPOSITE: *Bridesmaids' bouquets surround this lovely cake decorated with matching sugar flowers.*

Cake: Sylvia Weinstock. Photo: Fred Marcus Photography

ABOVE: *This exquisitely detailed silver base is the perfect complement for an elegant cake topped with a ribbon-draped bow.*

Cake: European Cake Gallery. Photo: Madearis Studio

RIGHT: *Hand-molded white flowers and ivy on a frosting-laced background. This delicious cake has a chocolate mousse filling and was designed by Sylvia Weinstock.*

Photo: Fred Marcus Photography

THIS GROOM'S CAKE WAS INSPIRED BY A DUCK POND IN
FRONT OF AN HISTORIC ESTATE. CAKE: JAN KISH.
PHOTO: JOHN W. CORBETT

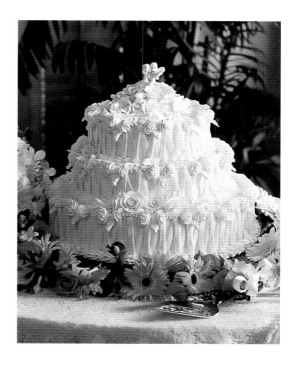

OPPOSITE: ABOVE LEFT: *A WHITE CHOCOLATE EIFFEL TOWER SITS ATOP THIS UNIQUE TWO TIERED CAKE DEPICTING THE COUNTRY OF FRANCE. PHOTO: ELIOT HOLTZMAN.*

ABOVE RIGHT: *INSPIRED BY THE VICTORIAN MANSION SELECTED FOR THE WEDDING RECEPTION, THIS CAKE IS ARTFULLY TRIMMED WITH RENAISSANCE-STYLE DETAILING AND TOPPED WITH A MINIATURE VASE OF FLOWERS CREATED FROM GUM PASTE. CAKE: THE CAKEWORKS. PHOTO: IMAGE EXPERTS.*

BELOW RIGHT: *A MASTERPIECE OF CARROT CAKE WAS THE PERFECT GROOM'S CAKE FOR THIS ARCHITECT GROOM. PHOTO: KEVIN HYDE*

THIS PAGE: ABOVE: *A MAJESTIC CAKE FOR A REGAL RECEPTION. CAKE: JAN KISH. PHOTO: LAMBERT PHOTOGRAPHY.* ABOVE RIGHT: *TASTEFULLY TRIMMED, THIS CAKE IS IDEAL FOR A SMALLER RECEPTION. PHOTO: DURANGO STEELE.* RIGHT: *"SATIN ELEGANCE" CAKE, DESIGNED BY COLETTE PETERS, RESEMBLES A STACK OF EXQUISITELY WRAPPED WEDDING GIFTS AND CLEVERLY REPLICATES THE ROWS OF PEARLS AND QUILTING THAT ACCENTED THE BRIDE'S GOWN. PHOTO: WITH PERMISSION, LITTLE BROWN AND CO. FROM COLETTE'S WEDDING CAKES BY COLETTE PETERS, 1995*

LEFT: *The smooth icing of this five-layer cake is enhanced by the intricately-domed crown.*

CAKE: JAN KISH. PHOTO: LAMBERT PHOTOGRAPHY

BELOW: *Precise floral detail makes this cake particularly engaging. Inspired by antique china pattern.*

CAKE: CILE BELLEFLEUR-BURBIDGE CAKES. PHOTOS: JOHN R. BURBIDGE

CAKE TOPS

A wedding cake is traditionally crowned with a cake top that may be whatever suits your fancy. In the past, it was most often a porcelain figure of a bride and groom. Some couples still desire a miniature pair atop their cake, and for those who do, beautiful crystal and porcelain figurines are available. Before you purchase one, however, ask your parents if they perhaps saved the cake top from their wedding cake. If so,

RIGHT: *A white masterpiece of sugar flowers and lattice work.*

CAKE: CILE BELLEFLEUR-BURBIDGE CAKES. PHOTO: JOHN R. BURBIDGE.

BELOW: *Tattinger prize-winning cake. Cake: Cile Bellefleur-Burbidge Cakes.*

PHOTO: JOHN W. CORBETT

consider using theirs. Cake tops from the forties, fifties, and sixties have a nostalgic charm. Many were lovely porcelain figurines, and your parents' cake top will have great sentimental value as well.

Other options are available for those couples who don't wish to use a bride-and-groom cake top. Fresh sugar flowers are always popular, mounded in a glorious arrangement or placed within a tiny gazebo. Sugar Bouquets' Rosemary Watson creates a vase of molded sugar that holds an extraordinary arrangement of miniature blossoms. Fortunately, it is easily preserved for many years, provided it's kept dry.

OPPOSITE: *An exquisite table draped in gold and ivory dupioni silk, by Floramor Studios, accents this stunning six-tiered fondant covered cake, decorated with cascading edible flowers and folded bows. Photo: Eliot Holtzman*

ABOVE: *Celestial elegance: gold-meshed ribbon spotlights the gold stars on this cake's smooth icing surface. Cake: Jan Kish. Photo: Lambert Photography*

RIGHT: *A white lace table treatment detailed with bows and green garlands complements this lovely cake of dotted Swiss and cascading roses. Photo: G. Gregory Geiger*

Other choices might include a pair of toasting glasses, tiny cherubs or love doves. In her designs, Jan Kish has used a pair of sugar anchors, a saxophone and trumpet, a scalloped seashell cradling two pearls, and even a blown-glass Mickey and Minnie Mouse.

THE CAKE TABLE

The cake table is the site where the rituals of the wedding cake unfold. In front of this display, you and your groom will cut the first slice of cake and feed it to each other. Your new union will then be heralded with the champagne toast. Cakes are usually displayed on a table or wheeled in on a cart after the meal has been served. In either case, the cake should be set off by flowers and greenery, an elegant cake knife and server, and a lovely tablecloth that complements the cake, and doesn't compete with it.

Think of the cake table as a tableau or display window, where every element combines to make a stunning overall impression. To showcase the cake, place a mirror behind the cake table. Couples who have their reception in the same location as the

ABOVE: *This cake designed by Jan Kish features a joyful cherub atop layers draped in creamy frosting and edible floral accents. Photo: Kent Smith.* RIGHT: *Crystal flutes, adorned with organza bows and a petite flower make wonderful toasting glasses. Beverly Clark Collection.*
OPPOSITE: *Cake by Jan Kish using sugar flowers, accented with ivy. Photo: John W. Corbett*

ABOVE: *Jan Kish duplicated the elaborate lace detail of this bride's gown on her wedding cake. Photo: David's Studio*
OPPOSITE: *Grand roses and corded bows sculpted of pastillage offer dramatic styling to this five-layer cake. Photo: James D. Macari*

ceremony often use the altar or chuppah area as a focal point for the cake.

THE GROOM'S CAKE

The groom's cake is generally viewed as an optional treat, although some bakers have noticed a resurgence in its popularity, particularly at the rehearsal dinner. Serving the cake at this event rather than at the wedding is a clever idea because it doesn't compete with the wedding cake. In the past the groom's cake was typically a fruitcake. Today, it is a flavor chosen by the groom, often designed to highlight his favorite pastime.

CHOOSING A BAKER

Wedding cake creators are known by various titles: pastry chef, wedding cake designer, and baker. To select a good one, follow the route you used in choosing the other professionals at your wedding. In addition, bridal magazines and bridal fairs are also good sources for your investigation and often you can sample the wares.

Many times, your caterer or reception site will provide the wedding cake. Since wedding cakes may not be their specialty, ask to see pictures and taste a cake you are considering. When your caterer or reception site provides the cake, the fee for slicing is usually included in the price. If you choose to purchase a cake from another source, you may incur an extra charge.

ORDERING YOUR WEDDING CAKE

Meet with a few bakers before selecting the one who will create your wedding cake. Arrange these interviews three or four months before the wedding. Bring items that will help the baker get a feel for the cake you want: photos of cakes you like, your dress, the flowers and colors that will be highlighted in your wedding.

ABOVE: *GIFT PACKAGE REPLICA CAKES ARE POPULAR AMONG COUPLES TODAY. THIS SMALL VERSION WITH A DARK CHOCOLATE GLAZE, TIED WITH STUNNING WHITE CHOCOLATE BOWS AND TRAILING RIBBONS IS IDEAL FOR A SMALL WEDDING SHOWER OR AS A GROOM'S CAKE. CAKE: CAKEWORK. PHOTO: PETER DIGGS*

LEFT: *WEDDING CAKE CHARMS . . . AN OLD SYMBOLIC TRADITION RETURNS. BRIDESMAIDS EACH SELECT A RIBBON AND PULL A CHARM FROM THE CAKE BEFORE IT IS CUT. THE CHARM SIGNIFIES THEIR FORTUNE. BEVERLY CLARK COLLECTION*

RIGHT: *MARBLED FROSTED TIER CAKE DECORATED WITH FLOWERS AND TWIGS. CAKE: CAKEWORK. PHOTO: PETER DIGGS*

Ask to see photographs from other weddings, and discover when you might sample some cakes. Bakers often set aside a certain date when samples of all of their flavors are available for couples to taste. Discuss the size of your guest list, a possible groom's cake, and the season and location of your wedding. Summer weddings, especially those held outdoors, may call for a type of cake and frosting that will hold up well in the heat.

Order your cake at least six to eight weeks before the wedding. At that time, you'll leave a deposit with the baker you have selected. Be sure to get a receipt or contract listing all the particulars of your order, including the date, time, and location of the delivery, the total price, and the balance due.

ABOVE: *Based on a popular Colette Peters' design, Diane Jacobs, of The Cakeworks, created her own adaptation of a gift box cake by alternating squares and rounds, with beautiful gold and cream embellishments.*
PHOTO: *Image Experts*

ABOVE RIGHT: *Graceful edible lilies atop this rolled fondant-covered cake.*
CAKE: *Cakework*

RIGHT: *Rich chocolate frosting ripples along the tiers of this four layer cake.*
PHOTO: *Durango Steele*

SAVING THE TOP TIER

Saving the top tier of the wedding cake is a time-honored custom. It began as one of the many superstitions surrounding newlyweds. If the cake crumbled before the first year had passed, it meant the marriage was in trouble. Today, refrigeration has altered the odds in your favor. Not only will your cake be preserved intact, there's a good chance it will be quite tasty

even after a year. If you'd rather enjoy the cake on your wedding day, consider saving a few slices instead of the entire top tier.

Make sure the portion of cake you are saving is securely wrapped and frozen immediately after the celebration. In addition, why not set aside a bottle of the champagne or wine you served at the reception? It's a memorable way to toast your first anniversary in the properly jubilant wedding spirit.

OPPOSITE FAR LEFT: *Duplicating the effect of fabric gathers, secured with pastillage flowers cascading down the layers.*
Cake: Jan Kish. Photo: Lance Parker
LEFT: *Wide pleats of fondant, gardenias, leaves and ribbons accented with tiny delicate pink roses. Cake: Cakework. Photo: Peter Diggs*
BELOW: *Fondant pleats are the surface for a cornucopia of Autumn-colored pastillage roses. Cake: Cakework. Photo: Peter Diggs*

THIS PAGE RIGHT: *This fabulous hat and hat box cake was created by using rolled fondant and pastillage. Cake: Colette Peters, author of Colette's Cakes.*
BELOW: *Hatbox cake, tied together with contrasting ribbons and accented with petite flowers. Cake: The Cakeworks.*

Bon Voyage

THE CELEBRATION of a lifetime, so meticulously planned, has all but ended, and the two of you are about to embark on your long-awaited honeymoon—that anticipated vacation where you and your new husband can relax together, alone at last. As you race past the guests amid a hail of rose petals, rice or bubbles your eyes will focus on the vehicle that stands ready to whisk the two of you away.

The traditional getaway car, trailing cans, shoes and decorated with paper roses, is still a favorite form of transportation from reception to destination. Some couples opt for the unusual exit—a horse-drawn carriage, a motor-cycle, an antique convertible, or even atop a fire truck. With a final triumphant wave, they bid farewell to the friends and families who have shared their joyful celebration.

Many brides and grooms ask only that their honeymoon be romantic and restful. They may choose to luxuriate aboard a cruise ship in the Caribbean or one that drifts past the Greek islands, or to linger a full two weeks in a tropical resort. Other couples plunge into an adventure, hiking the Blue Ridge Mountains or embarking on a whirlwind tour of Europe.

As you unwind in the first few days of your honeymoon, savor this special time. When you return home, a new life awaits you, but for now you and your husband are "newlyweds." Enjoy yourselves, get to know each other again, and together recall the unforgettable moments of your wedding day.

PREVIOUS PAGE: *Horse drawn carriage from Wedding Carriages.*

Photo: Bronson Photography

STEPHANIE HOGUE

STEPHANIE HOGUE

STEPHANIE HOGUE

257

Durango Steele

Durango Steele

PHILIPPE CHENG

DURANGO STEELE

PHILIPPE CHENG

DURANGO STEELE

263

SCOTT A. NELSON

BARON STAFFORD

JENNIFER DRAKE

CLAY BLACKMORE

MONTE CLAY

STEPHANIE HOGUE

PLANNING CALENDAR

The following checklist will help you and the groom organize your time to insure that you take care of all aspects of your wedding. These are general recommendations and should be adapted to your particular needs.

BRIDE'S CHECKLIST

Six to Twelve Months Before

- Select a wedding date and time.
- Make a preliminary budget.
- Determine your wedding theme or style.
- Reserve your ceremony and reception location.
- Determine who will officiate at the ceremony.
- Hire a wedding consultant, if you plan to use one.
- Decide on your color scheme.
- Determine the size of the guest list.
- Start compiling names and addresses of guests.
- Select bridal attendants.
- Have fiancé select his attendants.
- Plan reception.
- Check catering facilities, if at a club or hotel.
- Select a caterer, if one is necessary.

- Select a professional photographer and videographer.
- Select a professional florist.
- Select your dress and headpiece.
- Announce your engagement in the newspaper.
- Select bridesmaids' dresses.
- Select engagement ring with fiancé, if he has not already done so.

Four Months Before

- Make final arrangements for ceremony (deposits should be paid, contracts signed).
- Make sure all bridal attire is ordered.
- Have both mothers coordinate and select their dresses.
- Register at a bridal registry in the towns of both families.
- Order invitations and personal stationery.
- Complete the guest lists and compile them in order.
- Select the men's wedding attire and reserve the right sizes.
- Check requirements for blood test and marriage license in your state.
- Make appointment for physical exam.
- Shop for wedding rings.
- Start planning the honeymoon.
- Decide where you will live after the wedding.
- Begin shopping for trousseau.

Two Months Before

- Address invitations and announcements. They should be mailed four to six weeks before wedding.
- Finalize all details with caterer, photographer, florist, reception hall manager, musicians, etc.
- Order wedding cake, if not supplied by caterer.
- Finalize ceremony details with officiant.
- Make rehearsal arrangements.
- Plan rehearsal dinner.
- Plan bridesmaids' luncheon.
- Make appointments with hairdresser.
- Arrange accommodations for out-of-town attendants or guests.
- Finalize honeymoon plans.

One Month Before

- Have a final fitting for your gown and bridal attendants' gowns.
- Have a formal bridal portrait taken.
- Complete all physical or dental appointments.
- Get blood test and marriage license.

- Make transportation arrangements for the wedding day.
- Purchase gifts for attendants.
- Purchase gift for fiancé, if gifts are being exchanged.
- Have the bridesmaids' luncheon.
- Purchase going away outfit.
- Keep a careful record of all gifts received (write thank-you notes immediately instead of letting them pile up).
- Make sure you have all accessories, toasting goblets, ring pillow, garter, candles, etc.
- Select responsible person to handle guest book and determine its location.

Two Weeks Before

- Attend to business and legal details. Get necessary forms to change names on Social Security card, driver's license, insurance and medical plans, bank accounts; make a will.
- Prepare wedding announcements to be sent to newspaper.
- Reconfirm the accommodations for out-of-town guests.
- Arrange to have possessions and gifts moved to your new home. Give a change-of-address card to the post office.
- Finish addressing announcements to be mailed on the wedding day.

One Week Before

- Contact guests who have not responded.
- Give the final count to caterer and review details.
- Go over final details with all professional services you have engaged. Inform them of any changes.
- Give photographer the list of pictures you want.
- Give the videographer a list of shots you would like included in the video.
- Give all musicians the lists of music for the ceremony and reception.
- Plan the seating arrangements.
- Arrange for someone to assist with last-minute errands and to help you dress.
- Practice having your hair done to make sure it comes out properly, and determine the time it will take.
- Practice using your make-up in the same type of lighting you will have on the wedding date.
- Keep up with the writing of your thank-you notes.

- Pack your suitcase for the honeymoon.
- Make sure you have the marriage license.
- Make sure you have the wedding rings, and they fit.
- Make sure all wedding attire is picked up and fits properly.
- Have a rehearsal with all participants, reviewing their duties.
- Attend rehearsal dinner party. Stay calm and enjoy yourself.
- Stay with the family the night before the wedding. Get to bed early. You will want to look and feel great the next day.

On the Wedding Day

- Be sure to eat something. You have a big day ahead, and many brides have been known to faint.
- Take a nice relaxing bath.
- Fix hair or have an appointment to have it done at least three to four hours before the ceremony.
- Make sure nails are done. Allow plenty of time to apply make-up. Have all accessories together.
- Start dressing one to one-and-a-half hours before the ceremony. If pictures are being taken before the ceremony, then have yourself and attendants ready about two hours before the ceremony.
- Have the music start thirty minutes before ceremony.
- Have guests seated. Five minutes before the ceremony, have groom's parents seated. Immediately before procession, the bride's mother is seated and the aisle runner is rolled out.

After the Wedding

- Send announcement and wedding picture to newspapers.
- Mail announcements.
- Write and mail thank-you notes.

GROOM'S CHECKLIST

Six to Twelve Months Before

- Purchase the bride's engagement ring.
- Discuss with fiancée the date and type of wedding.
- Start on your guest list.
- Choose best man and ushers.

- Start planning and making necessary arrangements for the honeymoon.
- Discuss and plan with fiancée your new home together. If fiancée is moving in with you, start cleaning out closets, cupboards, and drawers to make room for your bride and wedding gifts.

Four Months Before

- Shop with fiancée for wedding rings.
- Complete your guest list, including full names, addresses and zip codes with phone numbers.
- Check requirements for blood test and marriage license in your state, or the state you are being married in.
- Select and order men's wedding attire with your fiancée.
- Finalize all honeymoon plans and send in deposits if required (don't delay—some resorts fill up fast in popular months).

Two Months Before

- Meet with officiant to finalize ceremony details.
- Assist parents with plans for the rehearsal dinner party.
- Discuss the amount and the financial arrangement for the flowers which are the groom's responsibility.
- Arrange accommodations for out-of-town attendants.

One Month Before

- See that all attendants have been fitted and wedding attire has been ordered.
- Purchase gifts for best man and ushers.
- Purchase wedding gift for fiancée, if gifts are being exchanged.
- Pick up wedding rings. Make sure they fit.
- Take care of business and legal affairs (add bride's name to insurance policies and medical plans, make a new will, add her name to joint checking account or joint charge cards). If you have both agreed to a pre-nuptial agreement, have it drawn up and signed.

Two Weeks Before

- Together with fiancée, gather necessary documents and get your marriage license.
- Arrange wedding day transportation.
- Reconfirm accommodations for out-of-town guests.
- If moving, give change-of-address card to post office; arrange to have utilities and phone

service turned on in the new home. If not moving, finish cleaning and reorganizing your home; help your fiancée move her things.
- Have your hair cut.

The Week Before

- Discuss all final details with fiancée; offer to assist if needed.
- Pick up and try on wedding attire.
- See that attendants get their wedding attire.
- Pack clothes for honeymoon.
- Reconfirm all honeymoon reservations.
- If flying, make sure you have plane tickets.
- See to it that you and your attendants are at the rehearsal and they know their duties.
- Go over special seating or pew cards with ushers.
- Arrange for gifts brought to the reception to be taken to your new home.
- Make sure luggage is in the car or the hotel where you will stay your first night.
- Attend rehearsal dinner. Relax and enjoy yourself.
- Get to bed early. You want to look and feel your best!

The Wedding Day

- Be sure to eat something in the morning.
- Allow plenty of time to get dressed (start one hour before ceremony).
- Get to the ceremony location on time!
- Give the best man the bride's wedding ring.
- Place the officiant's fee in a sealed envelope. Give it to the best man so he may present it after the ceremony. Don't forget to take the marriage license to the ceremony, or make sure the best man will bring it.
- Have the best man and maid of honor sign the wedding certificate as witnesses.
- At the wedding dance first with your bride, then with both mothers and the bridesmaids.
- Just before leaving the reception, thank the bride's parents, and say good-bye to your parents.

After the Wedding

- Make sure on the first day of the honeymoon to send flowers or a telegram expressing your appreciation and thanking the bride's parents again for a beautiful wedding and reception.

SOURCES

Wedding Photographers

ADAMS AND FAITH PHOTOGRAPHY
P.O. Box 5995
Portland, OR 97228
(503) 227-7850

GLENDA BACON CARTER
Carter Photography
575 Five Cities Drive, Suite 152
Pismo Beach, CA 93449
(805) 473-3434

BENNETT PHOTOGRAPHY
13888 Ransom Road
Moorpark, CA 93021
(805) 529-1240

BRONSON PHOTOGRAPHY
2060 Montrose Ave
Montrose, CA 91020
(818) 249-5864

PHILIPPE CHENG PHOTOGRAPHY
545 West 111th Street, Apt #1L
New York, NY 10025
(212) 678-1930

TOM AND LANI CHURCHILL
P.O. Box 463
Hana, HI 96713
(800) 349-8887

MONTE CLAY AND ASSOCIATES
Clay Blackmore
10887 Lockwood Drive
Silver Spring, MD 20901
(301) 593-3344

JOHN W. CORBETT
928 W. Main Road
Middletown, RI 02842
(401) 846-4861

DAVID'S STUDIO
David Everard
52 South High Street
Dublin, OH 43017
(614) 766-6700

PETER DIGGS
2711 18th Street #33
San Francisco, CA 94110
(415) 648-2266

JENNIFER DRAKE PHOTOGRAPHY
3644 San Gabriel Lane
Santa Barbara, CA 93105
(805) 569-9690

JOSHUA ETS-HOKIN
Ets-Hokin Studios

470 Potrero Avenue
San Francisco, CA 94110
(415) 255-8645

BRUCE FORRESTER PHOTOGRAPHY, INC.
809 Spring Drive
Mill Valley, CA 94941
(415) 388-3686

ALVIN GEE PHOTOGRAPHY, INC.
3300 South Gessner, Suite 120
Houston TX 77063
(713) 877-4038

G. GREGORY GEIGER, CPP
Gregeiger Co. Utd., Inc.
P.O. Box 943
Orange, CT 06477
(203) 795-8651
300 Brannan Street
San Francisco CA 94107
(415) 543-1755

CALVIN HAYES PHOTOGRAPHY
1325 Key Highway
Baltimore, MD 21230
(410) 685-0646

STEPHANIE HOGUE PHOTOGRAPHY
119 South Figueroa Street
Ventura, CA 93001
(805) 641-1055

ELIOT HOLTZMAN PHOTOGRAPHY
50 C Street
San Rafael, CA 94901
(415) 459-3980

KEVIN HYDE
Photographers of People, Ltd.
101 Merchants Drive
Norcross, GA 30093
(770) 414-5297

BRIAN KRAMER PHOTOGRAPHY
4416 Mammoth Avenue
Sherman Oaks, CA 91423
(800) 221-9022
(818) 907-1778

LAMBERT PHOTOGRAPHS
Nancy Lambert and
Judy Lambert Haydin
6756 Willow Grove Place
Dublin, OH 43017
(614) 766-9567

JAMES D. MACARI
925 De La Vina Street
Santa Barbara, CA 93101
(805) 965-3255

MADEARIS STUDIO
1304 West Abram
Arlington, TX 76013
(817) 277-0759

FRED MARCUS PHOTOGRAPHY, INC.
Andy Marcus

245 West 72nd Street
New York, NY 10023
(212) 873-5588

HEIDI MAURACHER PHOTOGRAPHY
133 East De La Guerra Street, # 373
Santa Barbara, CA 93101
(805) 965-6673

T.G. McCARY PHOTOGRAPHY
1207 Maine Street
Natchez, MS 39120
(601) 446-5670

RICHARD MILLER PHOTOGRAPHY
40 Great Circle Drive
Mill Valley, California 94941
(415) 388-3722

SCOTT A. NELSON PHOTOGRAPHY
7201 Haven Avenue, Suite E-145
Alta Loma, CA 91701
(800) 941-4003

PARKER PHOTOGRAPHS
Lance Parker
2740 Festival Lane
Dublin, OH 43017
(614) 766-7222

JOANN PECORARO (WADE)
Photography by Joann
150 El Sueno Road #F
Santa Barbara, CA 93110
(805) 967-2041

PORTRAITS BY TONY
825 Cedar Terrace
Dearfield IL 60015
(847) 940-7580

STEPHANIE RAE PHOTOGRAPHY
Stephanie Rae Munk
2724 Upper Cattle Creek Road
Carbondale, CO 81623
(970) 963-0333

DENIS REGGIE
75 14th Street
Atlanta, GA 30309
(404) 873-8080

JOHN REILLY PHOTOGRAPHY
358 West Ontario
Chicago, IL 60610
(312) 266-2550

KENT SMITH PHOTOGRAPHY
12923 Stonecreek Drive
Peckerington, OH 43147
(614) 866-1777

BARON ERIK SPAFFORD
1815 Gillespie Street
Santa Barbara, CA 93101
(805) 569-9939

DURANGO STEELE PHOTOGRAPHIC ARTIST
P.O. Box 1467
Santa Barbara, CA 93102
(805) 966-0521

P.O. Box 6002
Boulder, CO 80306
(303) 449-4240

WEDDINGS BY WEINTRAUB
432 South Pacific Coast Highway
Redondo Beach, CA 90277
(310) 316-1130

CLINT WIESMAN
Generations
122 West Figueroa Street
Santa Barbara, CA 93101
(805) 965-5649

Portraits

CHUCK GARDNER PHOTOGRAPHY
11362 Burnham Street
Los Angeles, CA 90049
(310) 472-0170

JACKY WINTER
411 Corona del Mar #A
Santa Barbara, CA 93103
(805) 963-3988

Contributing Commercial Photographers

AMEDEO
CRISTIANA CEPPAS
SIDNEY COOPER
CLARK CROUSE
MICHAEL GARLAND
HENRY HAMAMOTO
CLAUDIA KUNIN
DAVID SIEGLE
SCOTT STREIB

Stylist

SUNDAY HENDRICKSON

Cake Designers

CAKEWORK
Cecille Gady
613 York Street
San Francisco, CA 94110
(415) 821-1333

THE CAKEWORKS
Diane Jacobs
117 North LaBrea Avenue
Los Angeles, CA 90036
(213) 934-6515

CILE BELLEFLEUR-BURBIDGE
Cile Bellefleur Cakes
12 Stafford Road
Danvers, MA 01923
(508) 774-3514

CHRISTINE DAHL
1132 Vallecito Road
Carpinteria, CA 93013
(805) 684-5547

EUROPEAN CAKE GALLERY
844 North Crowley Road
Crowley, TX 76036
(817) 297-2240

FANTASY FROSTINGS
Joyce Maynor
10050 S. Mills Ave
Whittier, CA 90604
(310) 941-6266

JAN KISH
La Petite Fleur
P.O. Box 872
Worthington, OH 43085
(614) 848-5855

MONTECITO CONFECTIONS
Katie Scott
P.O. 42344
Santa Barbara, CA 93140
(805) 969-3383

PATTICAKES
Patricia Hinojosa
1900 North Allen Avenue
Altadena, CA 91001
(818) 794-1128

COLETTE PETERS
Colette's Wedding Cakes
327 West 11th Street
New York, NY 10014
(212) 366-6530

SUGAR BOUQUETS
Rosemary Watson
23 North Star Drive
Morristown, NJ 07960
(201) 538-3542

SYLVIA WEINSTOCK
273 Church Street
New York, NY 10013
(212) 925-6698

Invitations and Favors

MARGARET DiPIAZZA, INK
442 Third Avenue
New York, NY 10016
(212) 889-3057

ANN FIEDLER CREATIONS
333-1/2 South Robertson Boulevard
Beverly Hills, CA 90211
(310) 358-1177

ANNA GRIFFIN INVITATIONS
537 Armour Circle
Atlanta, GA 30324
(404) 817-8170

KEEPSAKES
Mona Montaz & Irma Caballero
4247 Canoga Ave
Woodland Hills, CA 91364
(818) 974-8964
(888) 540-5337

La Vie en Rose Studio
Catherine Titus
47 Brighton Court
Santa Rosa, CA 95403
(800) 585-9372
(707) 525-8278

ROCK SCISSOR PAPER
1525 Cardiff Avenue
Los Angeles, CA 90035
(310) 286-2845

WRAPPINGS
Joyce Gross
537 Armour Circle
Atlanta, GA 30324
(404) 815-0690

YESTERYEAR
Yolanda Tisdale
8816 Beverly Boulevard
Los Angeles, CA 90069
(310) 278-2008

Designers and Consultants

PARTY PERFECT
Sherri D. Minkin
15 Barnstable Court
Owinga Mills, MD 21117
(410) 356-7177

TANSEY DESIGN ASSOCIATES, INC.
232 West 30th Street
New York, NY 10001
(212) 594-2287

THOMAS AND THOMAS
21402 Park Brook
Katy, TX 77450
(713) 647-9641

VINTAGE PRODUCTIONS
Mary Litzsinger
3247 Ginko Court
Thousand Oaks, CA 91360
(805) 492-2114

Floral Designers

ATLAS FLORAL DECORATORS, INC.
46-12 70th Street
Woodside, NY 11377
(718) 457-4900

BARBARA TAYLOR FLORAL DESIGNS
222 Crest Road
Baltimore, MD 21209
(410) 542-2020

EVENTS AND FLORALS BY DESIGN
Clare Webber
4551 Fairbain Avenue
Oakland, CA 94619
(510) 261-8606

FLORAMOR STUDIOS
Laura Little
569 Seventh Street
San Francisco, CA 94103

(415) 864-0145

THE FLOWER BASKET
Charles Case
925 Boston Post Road, East
Westport, CT 06880
(203) 222-0206

THE FLOWER STUDIO
Janet Green
1640 19th Street
Santa Monica, CA 90404
(800) 760-2861

HEARTS BLOOM WEDDING FLOWERS
Joni Papay
Santa Barbara, CA 93101
(805) 962-1657

SCOTT HOGUE
S.R. Hogue and Company
1270 Coast Village Road
Montecito, CA 93108
(805) 969-1343

LAUREL'S CUSTOM FLORIST
Charles Gonzalez
7964 Melrose Avenue
Los Angeles, CA 90046
(213) 655-3466

NATURE'S DAUGHTER
Kathy Whalen
39 Palmerston Place
Basking Ridge, NJ 07920
(908) 221-0258

PHILIP BALOUN DESIGNS
340 West 55th Street
New York, NY 10019
(212) 307-1675

RENNY DESIGN FOR ENTERTAINING
505 Park Avenue
New York, NY 10022
(212) 288-7000

RON WENDT FLORAL AND EVENT DESIGN
245 W. 29th Street, 5th Floor
New York, NY 10001
(212) 290-2428

Beverages

THE CAPPUCCINO CONNECTION
Ken Cohen
P.O. Box 2592
Santa Barbara, CA 93120
(805) 969-7295

Transportation

WEDDING CARRIAGES
Bill and Arley Barton
518 Fairview Avenue
Arcadia, CA 91007
(818) 447-6693

THE GONDOLA GETAWAY
Mike O'Toole
5437 East Ocean Blvd.

Long Beach, CA 90803
(310) 433-9595

Butterfly Releases

THE BUTTERFLY COLLECTION
John R. White
P.O. Box 1535
Shafter, CA 93263
(805) 746-6047

SWALLOWTAIL FARMS
Jacob Groth
P.O. Box 17
Carmichael, CA 95609
(916) 332-2041

Destination Weddings

GATEHOUSE TRAVEL TOURS
Phil and Sandy Walker
761 Rancho Drive
Long Beach, CA 90815
(310) 599- 8483
http://www.globalpac.com/gatehouse

HEAVENLY HANA WEDDINGS
Katherine M. Acker
P.O. Box 2609
Wailuku, Maui, HI 96793
(808) 349-8887
(800) 349-8887

THE MAUI WEDDING LADY
Judi Green
P.O. Box 277-309
Kihei, HI 96753
(808) 879-8256
(800) 928-5885

A WEDDING MADE IN PARADISE
P.O. Box 986
Kihei, Maui, HI 96753
(800) 453-3440

Accessories and Attire

LA PETITE AFFAIRE
Call (510) 562-8100 for the store
nearest you.

PETER FOX SHOES
105 Thompson Street
New York, NY 10012
(212) 431-6359 and
712 Montana Ave
Santa Monica, CA 90403
(310) 393-9669

NANCY TAYLOR
Designer for Alencon
Mill Valley, CA
(415) 389-9408

BEVERLY CLARK COLLECTION, BRIDAL ACCESSORIES
Call (800) 888-6866 for the store
nearest you.

BRIAN KRAMER